# HEALING AGONY

# Healing Agony

*Re-Imagining Forgiveness*

STEPHEN CHERRY

continuum

**Continuum International Publishing Group**

The Tower Building
11 York Road
London SE1 7NX

80 Maiden Lane
Suite 704
New York NY 10038

www.continuumbooks.com



British Library Cataloguing-in-Publication Data
A catalogue record for this book is available from the British Library.

ISBN 978-1-4411-1938-4

Typeset by Fakenham Prepress Solutions, Fakenham, Norfolk NR21 8NN
Printed and bound in India

*But above all, the heart*
*Must bear the longest part.*

George Herbert

*For Maggie, with heartfelt thanks and love*

# CONTENTS

## CHAPTER 1

# You Can't Just Flip Your Feelings

I was sitting in an empty church with the mother of a boy who had been murdered a few days previously. Four people had just turned themselves in to the police. 'I don't have to forgive them, do I?' she whispered, holding my hand. 'It's too early, far too early to be thinking of forgiveness,' I said, squeezing her hand and hoping that the police family support officers would come back into the church to bring the conversation to an end, thinking that this was long enough with the vicar. I confess that it was psychology and not theology or ethics that had come to my rescue. My advice had boiled down to suggesting that forgiveness takes time.

There is truth in that – very important truth. But there is more to forgiveness than the passing of time, and yet in that moment I could not say what it was. I felt extremely uncomfortable, embarrassed that I had nothing wiser to suggest. She had no idea that I had written a PhD about forgiveness. There was a time when I had hoped that it would stand me in good stead should such a dreadful moment ever occur. I tried not to let it show but I was squirming within, because for years I had been studying forgiveness and yet all that study seemed to evaporate in this situation of acute pain and simple need.

This book is an attempt to bridge the gap between the experiences of those for whom forgiveness becomes an issue, or source of anxiety, and some of what has been written about it. One of the first academic papers I ever read on the subject described forgiveness as a generous venture of trust.[1] It is a very helpful way of putting it. But how do people whose lives have been shattered or hearts broken embark on such a venture? How do they keep going? What might be the role of those (a family member, minister or professional carer) who, for one reason or another, find themselves accompanying a person for whom such a venture seems both impossible and yet obligatory? How might we take part in such a venture so that we facilitate the empowerment and the healing of the victim? Also, how do we cope if we ourselves are that victim? These are some of the questions that lie behind the reflections in these pages. But there is also another level of issues, for I write this as a Christian priest.

My concern is not only to help people forward, but also encourage and enable them to make deeper spiritual and theological connections. There is no escape from the language of forgiveness in Christianity whether in the Scriptures, the worship, the sacraments or the ethics. Yet there is a gap in the pastoral theology, the careful thinking through of what we might say, do, or suggest, in situations where forgiveness seems important but impossible. I experienced this gap profoundly when trying to support that mother, and it was agonizing. But as I have reflected on it in subsequent years I have come to the conclusion that the agony was appropriate. Forgiveness is not an easy answer or a quick fix. It is agony. However, it is not merely agony – it is *healing agony*.

Perhaps that sounds a bit strong. Forgiveness, for Christian people at least, is something we hear so much about that we take it for granted. I recall very vividly the occasion when forgiveness first became interesting to me. It was not after a tragic or violent event, or a personal betrayal. There was no victim in this situation at all; it happened during the hush of a church service. Recently ordained, I was conducting a service of Holy Communion with reverence, enthusiasm and anxiety. Not yet used to doing this regularly, my senses were on full alert. I was saying every word with deliberate emphasis; freighting every gesture with ancient significance and generous warmth. Part way through the service the congregation said a prayer of confession: 'We confess that we have sinned in thought, word and deed.' When it concluded I stood to say the prayer of absolution with authority and love: 'Almighty God, who forgives all who truly repent, have mercy upon you, pardon and deliver you from all your sin.'

I was struck by the enormity of what I was saying, the awesome and earth shattering message that sins were forgiven. Yet as the words of absolution came to an end I noticed that the moment passed with only a mumbled 'Amen', and there was not much heart in it. This set me wondering. What *is* going on here? Surely there is something much more dramatic involved in being forgiven than this suggests. In human terms, forgiveness happens when someone who was once angry or resentful towards us lets it drop. 'Forgiveness,' I thought, 'is at the heart of the Christian faith; it's what it is all so earth-shatteringly about.' Yet here was a moment of forgiveness passing by with less excitement than might be occasioned by a change in the weather.

My exploration of forgiveness has involved reading many books and articles, endless conversations and some writing. I have also travelled, first to South Africa to get a deeper understanding of the Truth and Reconciliation Commission (TRC) and then to New York in the aftermath of the 9/11 disaster. In South Africa I met all sorts of inspiring people as I criss-crossed the old apartheid boundaries. South Africans love to talk and I was there to listen – that was a great combination. People were passionate and optimistic. It was time for change and people were dreaming dreams and launching projects to promote development and justice. But as I tried to tune in to the reconciliation processes of which we had heard so much through the international media, I found that some of my expectations were ill-formed.

First, there was a tiredness about the subject that I had not anticipated. I was not the first person from Europe or North America to go to South Africa to ask about forgiveness and reconciliation, and I found that an extremely understandable story-telling fatigue had set in. Second, at that time people were just beginning to suspect that the authorities would not deliver on the promise of compensation awarded through the TRC process. People had told their stories but after an initial cathartic euphoria were beginning to feel let down and despondent. This meant that the subjects of reconciliation and forgiveness were caught up with tension and disappointment.

I remember talking with a woman in Johannesburg who had been through the TRC process as a victim and told her story but was not the smiling icon of forgiveness that I had so naïvely expected. 'I told them,' she said, 'about how I was tortured and so on, and as a result nothing has happened. I have no job and I live in a shack. What makes it worse is that the man who tortured me still works at the police station.'

I learnt a million things in South Africa but some images stand out. First, that forgiveness is rarely as simple as it seems and that every forgiveness story will have hidden and difficult depths. Second, that the historical context of a forgiveness story is of great importance – not only what happened in the past but what happens in the future. Some of these truths were in the back of my mind as I sat in the church holding the hand of a woman whose son had so recently been murdered. Whatever else forgiveness might mean, in that situation the road ahead was not going to be easy or straightforward and the last thing she needed was a religious representative suggesting that it might be.

The Canadian academic Jill Scott recently wrote at the end of her substantial, original and brilliant book on the subject: 'I now realise that forgiveness cannot be made simple.'[2] It is a good conclusion to come to, especially if it dissuades some well-meaning people from suggesting that it can be. People who have been hurt, injured, betrayed or violated know in their hearts that forgiveness is not going to be simple or easy. They will very probably feel that it is impossible or unimaginable. Yet forgiveness is too important and powerful to be ignored or sidelined. According to Hannah Arendt it is the only way to solve the 'predicament of irreversibility'.[3] It frees us from being prisoners of the past or, as Richard Holloway has put it, 'walking the treadmill of the past'.[4] Desmond Tutu makes the same point by saying that there is no future without it.[5] Forgiveness is difficult, but vital and that's why I have spent untold time wrestling with the issues and trying to write something helpful and yet realistic about it.

My visit to New York also taught me a great deal, although there it was reconciliation that people wanted to discuss. However, there was one especially vivid lesson about forgiveness. One day I went to see a Liberian priest working in the Bronx. We sat in her office in the church hall, one of those offices full of all the leftovers from the latest church sale. 'Oh yes,' she said, 'reconciliation; that's a kind of octopus. It has many tentacles.' When it came to forgiveness she was just as vivid. She told me a story about a family in Liberia where there had been a murder of a child and the parents were instantly forgiving. She was very suspicious. 'You can't just *do* that,' she insisted. 'Forgiveness is not a pancake manoeuvre. You can't just flip your feelings.' That phrase has stayed with me ever since and has had a major influence on the way I have tried to support anyone who has been the victim of serious unjust harm. But if you can't just flip your feelings, what can you do? That is the question of forgiveness.[6]

In 1952 C. S. Lewis wrote in his best-selling *Mere Christianity*: 'Everyone says forgiveness is a lovely idea, until they have something to forgive...'[7] This was seven years after the end of the Second World War and Lewis felt that people were asking very serious and searching questions and would want to ask him how he would feel about forgiving the Gestapo if he were a Pole or Jew. He did not answer the question, saying it was too difficult. He suggests that we should begin our thinking about forgiveness closer to home, in particular with those with whom we relate more intimately and who, he implies, offend or hurt us less grievously.

I can understand why he says this. The question of how victims of outrageous atrocity forgive their perpetrators *is* an extremely difficult one. Moreover it calls into question the neat Christian equation between forgiving and being forgiven. But we should not assume that forgiveness at home is easy. All forgiveness that is truly forgiveness is difficult because it is a gracious and healing response to unjust hurt. As the psychotherapist Bernadine Bishop has wisely written, true forgiveness 'has to be the outcome of a struggle, anguish, fluctuation, conflict: a profound engagement with good and evil within and without the self, which leaves all changed'.[8] It is such true forgiveness which is our concern here. It's the only sort that is of interest to those for whom the word has become the most important and yet most impossible in their vocabulary.

## The Forgiveness Family

As part of my exploration of forgiveness, I once took part in a conference on theology, spirituality and mental health and ran a workshop on the subject of 'self-forgiveness'. Until preparing for that I had not taken the question of self-forgiveness very seriously. Influenced by ethical writers, it seemed to me that the idea of forgiveness could only make sense if the giver and receiver were *not* the same person. However, thinking more seriously about 'self-forgiveness' soon convinced me that 'forgiveness' is not one simple thing. It is perhaps more like a small family of different things, all of which resemble each other in important ways but are nonetheless not to be confused with each other. So in that conference I spoke about *divine-forgiveness*, *other-forgiveness* and *self-forgiveness* as three different types or varieties of forgiveness. Categorizing it in this way would have pleased the philosopher Ludwig Wittgenstein and has led me to conclude that it is helpful to think in terms of the 'forgiveness family'.

In the forgiveness family the forgiveness of God is, as it were, the great ancestor or progenitor. The forgiveness of one person by another, 'other forgiveness' or 'relational forgiveness', is the nuclear family (a family within a family). The great ancestor divine forgiveness also has other descendents but these are cousins of the nuclear family. They include things like 'self-forgiveness' and 'pardon'.

Although there is rarely complete consensus among academics I think it fair to say that most would want to distinguish quite clearly between pardoning and forgiving. Pardon refers to the remission of the penalty which an institution might impose on someone who breaks a rule. To forgive someone, on the other hand, is to do something more personal. People forgive those who have hurt them.[9] Whether or not self-forgiveness is a type or version of forgiveness, a legitimate member of the family, is a more contested issue. There is a strong argument that the word 'forgiveness' is being used metaphorically here and my own inclination is to agree with those who say that 'self-acceptance' is a more accurate term for the immensely important personal project of learning how to live with one's far from perfect self.[10]

## Stories, Not Case Studies

Throughout the book we will encounter and explore various forgiveness stories which are in the public domain. Although my summary is in each case very condensed, it is often more extensive than the treatment given to such stories when people write about forgiveness. This is partly because, as I have already made clear, it is no part of my intention to suggest that forgiveness is straightforward or easy. Nor is it any part of my plan here to write something that puts pressure on people who are struggling to forgive to 'get on with it'. Rather it is to open up some space where the depth and complexity of being a direct or indirect victim of serious harm might be explored with an appropriate balance of emotional sensitivity, spiritual wisdom and intellectual rigour.

To focus on stories, rather than, for example, principles or theories, has two important implications. The first is that when forgiveness is described in narrative form it necessarily happens across *time*. That forgiveness is a *process* is one of the insights that has been developed and reinforced as people have reflected on forgiveness from different perspectives in recent years. The second implication is that forgiveness stories can be as *complex* and *unpredictable* as any other set of stories. This is why I prefer to speak of forgiveness 'stories' rather than forgiveness 'case studies'. There is something enigmatic about forgiveness. It is not a straightforward, simple or unambiguous matter. It's just not the sort of thing about which we can easily find representative cases and model examples. That does not mean that there is no such thing as a forgiveness story; far from it. What it means is that you can't boil the story down to something like the essence of forgiveness.

I often wonder whether it is helpful to speak of the *journey* of forgiveness. In some ways it is because a journey takes time, as does forgiveness. It also involves moving from one place to another, which is also true, though in the case of a forgiveness journey it is often a metaphorical way of describing what happens within a person who forgives. The problem with thinking of forgiveness as a journey, however, is that it suggests that we know more about both the intended destination and the time that the journey might take than is often really the case. So, for me, 'forgiveness adventure' seems a better description. Though that is not quite right either, since 'adventure' suggests that there is a positive and exciting feel to what happens, which is far from the lived reality of many victims. I am sure, though, that forgiveness stories often have the quality of *exploration* in that they involve travelling through unknown, inhospitable and frightening territory for an indeterminate period to an uncertain destination.

In a memorable moment in Peter Shaffer's play *Gift of the Gorgon* a character called Helen challenges Edward, who is planning to write a play which extols a bloody form of vengeful justice as a response to an IRA bomb being detonated in a London department store. In Edward's view, some form of retribution is the only righteous and passionate response to the murder of innocent people in a bomb blast; the only way to achieve justice. But Helen speaks out to show him that passion for revenge is not the only spirited response to moral outrage:

> You go on about passion, Edward. But have you never realized that there are many, many kinds? – Including a passion to kill our own passion when it's wrong. I'm not just being clever. The truest, hardest, most adult passion isn't stamping and geeing ourselves up. It's refusing to be led by rage when we most want to be... No other being in the universe can change itself by conscious will: it is *our privilege alone*. To take out inch by inch this spear in our sides that goads us on and on to bloodshed – and still make sure it doesn't take our guts with it.[11]

Forgiving involves facing this most difficult of moral and personal challenges: striving to take the goad from our sides without eviscerating ourselves of our guts – our moral sensibilities, our self-respect, our standards and our hopes. Helen calls this 'the passion to kill our own passion'. It is emphatically not about failing to have a moral, emotional and possibly heartrendingly painful response to being hurt or seeing others hurt. It is about actually having and experiencing this response and finding a better way forward than rage, revenge, bitterness or grudge. It involves not being captured in our own hurt, not being defined by those who have damaged us and not being broken by the burden of our own victimhood.

## Notes

1. Kolnai, A. 'Forgiveness', p. 102.
2. Scott, J. *A Poetics of Forgiveness*, pp. 200–201.
3. Arendt, H. *The Human Condition*, p. 237.
4. Holloway, R. *On Forgiveness,* p. 53.
5. Tutu, D. *No Future Without Forgiveness.*
6. One reader of a draft of this chapter challenged me about this. He had two comments. First, sometimes we *can* flip our feelings and second, there are

occasions when our feelings do seem to flip regardless of our intentions. I accept both points. I remain unconvinced, however, that forgiveness is often experienced as an intentional flip of the feelings and absolutely unconvinced that the role of the companion or one who is supporting someone who is struggling with forgiveness is to suggest, urge or insist that they attempt the pancake manoeuvre. You could say in fact that this book is for those for whom the pancake manoeuvre is impossible, unlikely or even unattractive but who still somehow live both with their pain and with the word 'forgiveness'.

7. Lewis, C. *Mere Christianity*, p. 101.
8. Bishop, B. 'The Visage of Offence', p. 30.
9. Unlike forgiveness, pardon does not have to do with the ameliorating or modifying of the emotions or attitudes of one who has been hurt. When someone is 'pardoned' what happens is that a punishment or penalty is waived by an office-holder who has the authority to speak in the name of some larger institution (the example often given is the President of the golf club). The point is that the pardoner is not the victim of the transgression but is responsible for the ongoing customs, rules or laws of the intuition or community or state. Pardon deals with the consequences of an offence not by a victim but by an objective judge.
10. See Vitz, P. C. and Meade, J. M. 'Self-forgiveness in Psychology and Psychotherapy: A Critique'. The authors propose that, 'self-forgiveness is a misleading and inaccurate concept for understanding the conditions to which it is applied', concluding that 'self-acceptance is a more accurate and useful term for the process and benefits attributed to self-forgiveness' (p. 248). They also 'strongly suggest that self-acceptance be substituted for the term "self-forgiveness" because the use of the word "forgiveness" inaccurately suggests that other and self-forgiveness have much more in common than is the case' (p. 261).
11. Shaffer, P. *The Gift of the Gorgon*, pp. 56–57.

CHAPTER 2

# The Wilderness of Hurt

It is one of the saddest and truest facts of life that when people are unjustly offended or injured they suffer several layers of consequence. Some of these are obvious. If you are maimed in a bombing you might well carry the injury, pain and disability for the rest of your days. If you are bereaved by a murder you remain bereaved long after the murderer has served a life sentence. These facts are well known and objective. The subjective side of things is more hidden. For instance, when people are the victims of a random crime, they often suffer a drop in self-esteem and self-confidence. People are ashamed when they are bullied or violated by someone who holds power over them. Paradoxically, when people are victims of a crime committed by someone they know, they may experience guilt or shame themselves.

The simplest and commonest word for the subjective consequences of being offended against is the little word *hurt*. Often when we say that we are hurt, we do not only mean that we have had pain inflicted on us but that the pain has somehow got *into* us. It has got past our defences and into our feelings and attitudes. In some cases, the hurt can even begin to infiltrate our sense of identity and undermine who we think we are. Hurt can dislocate, fragment or even shatter us. It takes us to the wilderness, a place of aridity and desolation, but also, in

Christian spirituality at least, to a place where struggle can be rewarded with wisdom and hope.

People are always hurt when a person or institution in which they trust lets them down. We know that it makes us vulnerable to trust someone else and that perhaps is why we expect people to respect the fact that we trust them. It is so obvious that we can only live by trusting people that we do not even notice that we are doing it. We get on the bus and, while the driver will want to see our ticket, we will not ask to see her driving licence. We go to a café and eat food from a kitchen that we have never seen. We walk along the cliff edge or pier trusting that no stranger will push us off.

Many have argued that we live in a relatively untrusting world these days, but the reality is that we cannot avoid placing trust in a number of people in order to get through a normal day. We give our trust to those with whom we share our lives and our deeper feelings: spouses and children, caring professionals and those who have access to confidential information about us. According to the psychologist Eric Erickson, personality development depends on resolving a series of basic conflicts. He argues that the first of these, which takes place in infancy, is between 'trust and mistrust'. Trust develops in response to reliability, care and affection. In response to these we develop 'trust' as the foundation stone of a healthy and functioning personality. Our capacity to trust is precious. It matters profoundly when it is broken.

In 1982 Denise Green's eighteen-month-old son died in Alder Hey hospital. After his death, in common with a lot of other children, his organs were removed from his body without parental consent being sought. Green discovered this five years after the event by reading about it in a newspaper article. When she phoned the hospital she was told in a matter of fact way: 'We have his brain, his lungs, his spleen, his liver, his kidneys, his intestines, and his reproductive organs.' Over the following years the Green family held two more burial services for William. This, however, did not prevent feelings of anger and bitterness welling up. No one was prosecuted. 'Justice hadn't been done, and people felt let down.'[1]

Looking at this in the context of stories of abuse or murder, one might be inclined to think that this is a relatively mild offence. Certainly it would have been a very different story if William's death had been caused by the negligence of the hospital staff. It is important, however, to recognize the depths of this situation. The deeper issues here arise from the breaking of trust. Denise Green does not tell us what her response was to the matter-of-fact phone call at the time. We do not know whether it was disbelief, shock, anger, a combination thereof, or other responses. What we do know is that a few years down the line she could hear the bitterness and anger in other people whose trust had been broken and that she recognized the destructive power in that. 'I did not want to go down that road,' she said, explaining how she came to choose and walk the path of forgiveness. 'What happened is out of my control, but how I respond is within my control.'

We are often provoked and discomforted when we begin to discern unattractive traits and attitudes in ourselves. As Mary Foley, a woman who decided to forgive the young woman who murdered her daughter in a stabbing incident in London, put it: 'I knew that if I didn't forgive, anger and bitterness would turn me into a person Charlotte [her murdered daughter] would not have liked, or my family and friends for that matter.'[2] People like Mary are self-aware and perceptive enough to see that the hurt they are feeling has begun to impact on who they are. Such development in self-awareness after being deeply hurt is not uncommon, but neither is it inevitable.

One of the subtle things about being unjustly hurt is that it can rob us of some of our self-awareness. This can be paradoxical and might go hand in hand with a high degree of self-consciousness, even self-absorption, because when we are deeply hurt we often turn in on ourselves. Such 'turning in' is a natural consequence of experiencing pain. Physical pain demands our attention, and so does 'hurt'. It draws us into ourselves. It can go the other way, of course. When hurt, we can become angry and focus our attention on the one who has hurt us and seek to hurt him or her in return. But either way it seems that we have moved to a more reactive mode and lost something of our selves.

This is a powerful cocktail of responses which, when taken together, can very quickly threaten to make us a different person. Once we were self-aware, interested in others, kind and engaging, but, having been deeply and unjustly hurt, our thoughts return again and again to the most unpleasant of reflections and inevitably these begin to impact on our demeanour, our words, our attitudes and our relationships. Whether we become aware that this is happening is far from certain, indeed it is unlikely that we ever fully realize how having been hurt impacts on the way we are with and to others. But, as Mary Foley has made clear, the journey towards forgiveness can begin precisely when we become aware of the longer-term damage that is being done to us, when we recognize some of the deeper consequences of having been unjustly hurt.

## Levels of Hurt

One of the reasons that forgiveness is difficult and enigmatic is that we ask the word, the concept or the process to do a lot of work for us. We want it to be relevant in quite different situations. Consider these:

- Someone accidentally bumps into you in the street.
- Someone steals your purse.
- Your spouse has an affair with your colleague.
- Someone you love is murdered.
- You are tortured.

We react in different ways to different events, but the word 'forgiveness' can be used to describe the way in which we move on from our own initial response in all of them. When we realize that this one word is potentially relevant in such a variety of situations we may begin to feel that it is overworking, trying to do too much. Once we recognize that the word 'forgiveness' is expected to apply to such different situations, we appreciate why it is that we find it difficult to understand. If we don't know what it means, we assume that it is going to be very hard to practise. This also explains why, if we look up a list of quotes about forgiveness, we do not find that the concept gets narrowed down but, rather, it seems to open up.

Towards the end of his first book on this subject, *Forgiveness and Christian Ethics*, Anthony Bash suggests that there are *varieties* of forgiveness.[3] He also suggests that while we can easily recognize forgiveness when it happens, forgiveness itself is not 'something that is clear cut'. Bash develops this line of thinking in his second book *Just Forgiveness*, where he distinguishes between 'thick' and 'thin' forgiveness: thick being 'robust and richly textured' and thin being 'rather less, while, nevertheless, still forgiveness'.[4] However, according to Bash, most forgiveness will be neither thick nor thin but somewhere in-between, so he speaks of a 'spectrum of responses'. There is also a spectrum of hurt.

Perhaps we should say that, just as there is no simple answer to the question of what forgiveness is, so also there is no one forgiveness process. Nor yet is there one answer to the question of what should or will happen next in a situation that seems to invite forgiveness. Forgiveness really is a difficult and complicated business. We not only need to break it down in order to understand it but we also need to be prepared to accept that it will never become 'clear cut'. That is, we need to engage with it *both* analytically *and* imaginatively. To help us do this I want to suggest that we think in terms of four different levels of hurt which people might inflict on each other: the *trivial*, the *serious*, the *significant* and the *shattering*.

The first level is that of the *trivial*. At this level even the word 'hurt' can seem like an overstatement. The harm involved is minor, incidental and often unintentional. These are incidents that are not only tolerable but should be tolerated. The second level is that of *serious or real* hurt. At this level we encounter things that are unjust and harmful but without terrible consequences: the theft of a small amount of money; an annoying deception; being let down by someone who is normally reliable. These are events that might reasonably cause us to pause and say 'no that was not right' but they do not significantly disorient or distress us once the initial shock or disappointment has worn off.

*Significant or painful* hurt happens at the next level. This is where we feel the injustice with pain, bewilderment, indignation or sadness. Forgiving at this level is more complex than at the second level because there are difficult psychological responses here: the offence has hurt and provoked us deeply. Perhaps we are angry, or indignant, or resentful, or confused and bewildered, or sad and despondent. Ethically, the situation might not be so different to the second level, just a matter of degree, but psychologically it is different and difficult. The difference between the second and third levels is not unlike

Bash's distinction between thin and thick forgiveness. It is not a cast-iron distinction, but it seems reasonable to distinguish those injuries which have a significant emotional impact from those which are less complex to live with, even if unjust.

The fourth level is different in quality and type to the others. It represents the level of major unjust harm – of *shattering* experience. At this level something has happened which undermines the health, integrity or identity of the victim. It is at this level that it seems impossible and outrageous to forgive and yet it is often when people are thus 'shattered' that the question of forgiveness seems to be most pressing and urgent.

Returning to the list of offences we considered earlier, different people might locate them at different levels. Thus the 'bump in the street' is at the first or trivial level. Having your purse stolen is more than trivial. It is significant, but however troublesome it might be we know that it might have been worse. We are not likely to be disoriented or uncontrollably distressed. The element of betrayal involved in the affair of a spouse with a colleague means that it is more than 'serious'. It is experienced as a level three offence, the level at which there is real emotional distress, disorientation and pain. Some, however, might find it to be a level four matter, as it undermines and 'shatters' the sense of self.

Moving on to the example of being tortured or having a loved one murdered we are certainly in the company of the desperately wounded and broken. Torture is, as we shall see, intended to break a person down psychologically, and so we should expect the victim of torture to be 'shattered'. But whether or not this is a more or less shattering experience than discovering that a loved one has been murdered is, of course, an impossible question to answer.

I am seeking to draw attention to two important points here. First that the word 'forgiveness' might be used across a range of situations from the trivial to the most serious. Second, that questions of forgiveness are framed not in relation to the objective offence (harm) but with regard to the subjective experience (hurt) that the offence precipitates. Forgiveness is a response to the hurt we have received, which is a consequence of the harm we have experienced. But different harms hurt different people in different ways.

Looking at the four levels in a little more detail it seems that, at level one, things happen that are not quite as we might like but that they are of no real moral significance and so the only wise thing to do is ignore them, or use them as an occasion for 'polite forgiveness'. If someone apologizes for mildly inconveniencing us through thoughtlessness or lack of circumspection we readily forgive. Similarly, if we ask to be forgiven because we feel we have to make an uncomfortable point to a colleague or to say something controversial in a meeting, we do so assuming that our request will be granted without question. But this is merely polite forgiveness. It has nothing to do with injustice, guilt or anger.[5]

To use the word 'forgiveness' in such situations is perhaps unfortunate, as it risks devaluing the currency. The word 'sorry' has almost come into disrepute because people use it so frequently in situations where there is no cause for sorrow.[6] But as long as it is kept in proportion, this use of it is benign, serving as a way of expressing our respect for the people whom we are inconveniencing or upsetting and replacing the older cliché, 'with great respect . . .' It is wrong, however, to confuse this sort of forgiving, or such use of the word 'sorry', with that which belongs at the other levels, because at each of them there is a moral issue, a matter of injustice, that needs to be addressed.[7]

The second and third levels have a great deal in common as ethically they differ from each other only in degree. Second level or 'serious' hurts are not trivial. If we have something stolen, or if we are slandered or treated unfairly then we might decide to ignore it, avenge it or forgive it. These are the three options before us and different people take different routes at different times. The way in which the second level differs from the third is that at the second level the offence, while unjust, is not distressing or disorienting. There might be an emotional aspect to the way in which someone responds to being offended at this level but it will not be the sort of response that is difficult for anyone to live with. At the third level, on the other hand, we encounter situations where the unjustly harmed person has been hurt to such a degree that their experience has a strong or even predominantly emotional quality. In the simplest case, what has happened has made them very *cross*. In many cases, however, there will be quite a cocktail of emotions in our response, reflecting both the nature and depth of the hurt and also something of who we are.

Thus, in the example given, 'your spouse has an affair' there is possibly some righteous anger or resentment. But those will not be the only emotions. There may also be feelings such as disappointment, jealousy, self-recrimination, guilt and many others, and different people will have different clusters of feelings all appearing in different orders and varying proportions or strengths.

But if that is true of the third level, it is even more the case with the fourth level where we encounter unjust suffering which is absolutely beyond our experience or imagination or capacity to cope. Here, the victim's experience is of overwhelming and disorienting trauma. At this level, people's experiences have undermined them and possibly even robbed them of the vary capacities which might enable or allow them to imagine forgiving.[8]

I have introduced the idea of levels of hurt to suggest that while we might talk about forgiving in one situation as something that might be expected, in another it might be difficult or even impossible. While the word 'forgiveness' is correctly used in several cases, the reality to which it can refer might be quite different, just as the experience of victims of various harms might be quite different. At level one, however, the word 'victim' seems too serious a word and so too does 'forgiveness'. It is the level of minor inconvenience accidentally inflicted and what is called for is not forgiveness, but tolerance. We will not consider the question of tolerance in any more detail here and mention it now only to clarify something that is *not* the same as forgiving. In order for a person to forgive they must first have been unjustly harmed and experience some level of hurt. Levels two, three and four therefore begin to describe the different types of hurt, different degrees of unjust harm, different situations, in which forgiveness might be relevant.

Let me emphasize two points. First, that the four levels are not objective but subjective and that in lived experience they will overlap in curious ways. Second, that we should expect the level of hurt endured to make a real difference to the way in which the challenge to forgive is experienced and to the kind of response that is possible. These are not the only factors relevant to forgiveness, but to neglect them is to fail to understand what might be involved in forgiving in any particular case.

## Forgiveness and the Will

One of the realities that people encounter after being seriously hurt or experiencing a significant loss is that they are muddled and bewildered. They may experience a kind of numbness until, after a while, it begins to wear off and be replaced, perhaps by quite sharp feelings. During the period of numbness (and perhaps well beyond it) the victim might not be at all clear about what they do actually want. So questions of will and desire are not far from the surface in the aftermath of harm – in the wilderness of hurt.

This leads to complications that need to be taken into account as we try to understand forgiveness. On the one hand, it seems to be absolutely the case that true forgiveness must come from the heart and that it must come freely. You cannot force someone to forgive – that would be absurd. We can only say 'we forgive' if we know that we are free *not* to forgive. It cannot be called forgiveness if it is a constrained or required response. Forgiveness is a gift. Jill Scott goes so far as to coin the word 'forgifting' to emphasize this.[9] But if forgiveness must come from the heart, and we can only forgive if we want to forgive, then does it follow that we can forgive by dint of will, that we can, so to speak, force ourselves to forgive?

Any attempt to answer, or live with, this question needs to take into account the reality of the divided will, the muddled mind. Clarity, integrity, constancy and steadfastness of purpose are all admirable qualities and virtues but they do not often characterize the state of mind of someone who has been harmed at anything above the trivial level. There are varying degrees of shock involved for all victims and this means that victims are rarely quite themselves. They may not be 'shattered' but they may well be confused and that confusion will often extend to what they want or desire. Part of the reality of being a certain kind of victim, or a victim with a certain, often Christian, psychosocial make up (you might say a Christian heart or soul) is precisely this confusion of volition. The victim is not sure what they want.

So in the aftermath of harm, a victim might experience acute indignation *and, at the same time*, the desire to forgive. But even to put it like this is to oversimplify. What I have called 'acute indignation' might be a variety of negative responses ranging from rage to resentment and the 'desire to forgive' might be more or less heartfelt and straightforward. One person might really want to forgive and yet feel overwhelmed by grief and anger, whereas another person might feel righteous indignation and yet also have a twang of guilt about it as they have in the back of their mind the thought that they really ought to be more forgiving.

The moral tension that people experience after hurt is part of the victim's agony and is integral to an ethical or spiritual commitment that values forgiveness. If your moral code is to take revenge, then there is no need to agonize. You simply plan and execute your reprisal. If it is a matter of retributive justice the only question is the appropriate punishment. If you are not concerned about matters of justice, or do not believe that you are worthy of being treated with dignity or respect, then equally you have no tension, you simply tolerate what has happened. But forgiveness involves exactly this internal tension, this wrestling within.

When trying to understand the question of the role of the will or personal desire in forgiveness, therefore, it is important to recognize that the situation is most unlikely to be straightforward. To suggest that forgiveness is *simply* an act of will is to fail to recognize that it is possible to want to forgive and yet find it impossible to do so. But as we ascend the levels of harm it becomes more and more likely that this is the case. Take the example of the mother of the murdered teenager beginning to think about forgiveness even in the earliest days of her grief. When people are hurt in a deep way, forgiveness becomes important and yet unimaginable, at precisely the same moment.

What this suggests is that while forgiveness is a matter of the will, in as much as it seems odd to suggest that you forgive against your own will, it is not *simply* a matter of the will. The victim of unjust harm is always placed in a complex ethical situation; the more serious the harm the more agonizing the situation. To suggest that there is something called 'forgiveness' which can somehow deal with all this and return things as far as possible to the state they were in before the offence, injury or violation occurred is unrealistic and naïve. Yet the word 'forgiveness' and the hope it signifies, will not go away.

## After Trauma

When people reflect and write about forgiveness they often use the word 'injury' or 'offence' to describe what has happened to the victim. These words, however, do not adequately describe the higher levels of harm, especially those which are 'shattering' and it is precisely these shattering experiences that are experienced as 'unforgivable'. They do something so disturbing to the victim, so shattering, that any talk of forgiveness can sound naïve and inappropriate. They are the kinds of experiences that seem to be entirely negative and irredeemable.

To begin to understand what happens to people who are harmed and hurt at this level, it can be helpful to reflect for a moment on Nietzsche's famous remark: 'What does not kill me makes me stronger.' What Nietzsche was reflecting here was the view that difficult experiences can facilitate the growth of virtues of strength – 'character-forming experiences'. Certainly they exist. They are unpleasant at the time and challenge us deeply. But they also enable us to develop the resources to cope better and more easily on another occasion. Certain disappointments might be like this, as might receiving poor feedback on our performance in some significant task. Having a 'near miss' when driving too quickly or taking a risk while walking in the mountains might help us to be more prudent. Getting soaked with rain every now and then while young makes us both hardy and inclines us to pack some waterproofs.

Such experiences as these do not kill us. They incline us to grow in virtue, which is to become stronger, better adapted, more able to cope, wiser, and so forth. But it is naïve to assume that, because some experiences are strengthening in one of a number of possible ways, the same can be said for all difficulties that do not quite kill us. In particular, it fails to do justice to the effects of extreme human cruelty and to the deep vulnerability of each and every human being, relationship and community.

So, despite Nietzsche's bold aphorism, some experiences actually weaken, wound and damage very deeply. We might cope but we are also wounded and more fragile. Such experiences can involve a degree of humiliation or degradation which is so profound that the self cannot recover its integrity. Torture is the obvious and extreme example. It is not as uncommon as it should be. Other situations of a more ongoing or chronic nature might also be like this. I am thinking of long-term bullying, being subject to the abuse of a more powerful person in the playground, in the park, at home or at work over an extended period, and also of political, social or economic oppression. Such scenarios give the lie to the naïvety of Nietzsche's famous remark. They need to be understood within a framework which involves both personal healing and the cessation of the oppressive conditions or the bullying behaviour; both of which are fundamental to situations in which we might be motivated to try to forgive – or at least feel that we have some duty in that regard, even if forgiving itself is beyond our imagination.

Torture, violent attack, years of child abuse or bullying are the kinds of experiences that can undermine and shatter aspects of the victim's core being, if not their whole self. But shattering experiences can also occur within the apparently more peaceful and promising environment of intimate relationships that have over the years been loving and trusting. These are the contexts of which Beverly Flanigan writes in her book *Forgiving the Unforgivable*.

Thinking within the context of existing relationships, she suggests that things that are 'unforgivable' often begin as 'events' which are experienced as significant 'injuries'. Thus they could be 'a lie, an affair, a sexual assault, or the violation of a promise'.[10] Whether or not any of these becomes 'unforgivable' depends on how things develop. In her first scenario there is repentance and forgiveness. In the second there is a gradual break-up of the relationship through a process she calls 'false reconciliation'. And in the third there is 'unforgivable injury' which she describes as 'a profound and irreversible assault on the fundamental belief system of the person who has been injured'. She explains it more fully:

> An injury that alters a moral history and ruptures a relationship begins with an event that violates a moral rule but does not stop there. Instead, it spirals on to violate other beliefs of the injured person, destroying in its wake belief after belief until the wounded person, too, is nearly destroyed.[11]

It might seem, from an objective perspective, that when certain rules or expectations are violated within a close relationship that this is the nub of the matter. However, from the victim's perspective it looks and feels very different. The particular nature of the offence is not the issue. What is at issue, what has been violated, is the trust, the heart of the relationship itself. When people are betrayed they take this sense of violation into themselves and it undermines many aspects of who they are. Self-respect is only part of it; self-confidence takes a big blow too. People even begin to mistrust their own personal life story. This is one of the commonest and cruellest aspects of betrayal. Everything seemed to be good; trust, love and respect seemed to be mutual. But the betraying event, or series of events, has cast all this in a new light. The victim is undermined by the betrayal in such a way as to make them the kind of person who is incapable of forgiving. It's not that the betrayer can't be forgiven but that the victim has lost the capacity to forgive.

It is important to underline, however, that this loss is not the fault of the betrayed. It is a consequence of having been betrayed. Anyone helping such a person, and the experience is not uncommon, needs to be aware both that this is likely to be the case and that, realizing that it is the case, the betrayed person's anguish will be increased. Where was once trusting love is now a sense of hurt and, possibly, rapidly developing hatred. It is an extremely uncomfortable and unpleasant place to be. The capacity to forgive, which is important in keeping and sustaining any relationship of love, seems to have been destroyed. A part of the self has died and this adds to the sense of loss. It is this subtle and poisonous combination which makes betrayal an example, not of injury or offence, but of trauma and violation.

## Notes

1. These quotations and all others in this section come from stories recorded by *The Forgiveness Project*. Denise Green's story can be accessed at http://theforgivenessproject.com/stories/denise-green-england/.
2. http://theforgivenessproject.com/stories/mary-foley-england/.
3. Bash, A. *Forgiveness and Christian Ethics*, pp. 159–173.

4. Bash, A. *Just Forgiveness,* p. 37.
5. This is perhaps an oversimplification. If someone pushes a trolley into your ankle causing sharp pain while using their mobile phone you might well be angry. But this would be a different level of hurt. What we are talking about at this level are the minor irritations of everyday life, not the painful consequences of another's irresponsibility, which would belong at level two or above depending on the degree of both pain and negligence. To have one's body seriously damaged by an irresponsible car driver – say drunk, speeding and using a mobile phone might take one to level four.
6. Davidson, M. *Sorry,* for instance, 'we tell ourselves that if only someone says sorry, everything will be all right and we can live happily ever after', p. x.
7. At the first level we only have two options – to ignore or to avenge. To avenge what is merely inconvenient or irritating is simply intolerant and not to be praised, encouraged or even perhaps tolerated. But to seek to *forgive* those who have annoyed us but not done anything unjust is also a serious error. It is to be a bit pompous. For where there is no injustice there is nothing to forgive. People might sensibly ask forgiveness for that which is upsetting but actually to try to forgive them for it is to fail to understand what is going on. When people ask for forgiveness at this level we should respond by agreeing, but what this means is that we simply tolerate.
8. Some people might be traumatized more easily than others, and some might be able to shake off the impact of the tragedies and violations that many might never come to terms with. However, it is responsible to expect and encourage people to have a proportional and appropriate emotional response to their experiences as this is one of the ways by which human beings form ethical communities and societies. We are, in a sense, right to be 'shattered' if we are 'violated'.
9. '*Forgifting* is a never-ending dance of producing and exchanging meanings, chipping away at resentment, and edging towards the other.' Scott, J. '*Forgifting*: Poetic and Performative Forgiveness in the South African Truth and Reconciliation Commission' p. 215. In making this point she is drawing on Julia Kriteva's insistence that forgiveness (or in French 'par-don') is about what we do *through giving.*
10. Flanigan, B. *Forgiving the Unforgivable,* p. 22.
11. Flanigan, B. *Forgiving the Unforgivable,* p. 26.

# CHAPTER 3

# After Torture

In the 1990s a play called *Death and the Maiden* had an extremely successful run in the West End of London. Written by the Chilean writer Ariel Dorfman, it was subsequently made into a film by Roman Polanski. The question on which the drama turns is this. If you are a victim of torture and subsequently find your torturer in your power, and there are no witnesses, what do you do? Indeed, what do you want, what do you need from your former torturer?

In the play, Paula, a victim of torture, finds herself in exactly this situation. She runs through all the possibilities. She first likes the idea of revenge: to inflict the same torture on her torturer as she had experienced 'systematically, minute by minute, instrument by instrument'.[1] But that desire is eventually superseded by the desire to hear him confess: 'I want him to sit down in front of the cassette recorder and tell me what he did... and then to have him write out in his own handwriting and sign it and I would keep a copy forever.'[2] As the play progresses she does make him confess but as he does so two things serve to make Paula's position even more excruciating.

First, she feels there is no hint of sorrow or regret in his words, and indeed he disowns them as soon as she threatens to kill him. However, in his confession he mentions details that Paula knows that only her torturer could have known. She realizes that she has in front of her the man who is definitely her torturer, who has confessed in full but who is not repentant. She threatens to shoot him and begins to count to ten. At 'nine' the curtain comes down. It is a large mirror inviting the audience to reflect on what they see in it. The play offers no easy answers because there are no easy answers. But it does frame one particularly agonizing question about forgiving. What do you do if you have power of life and death over someone who once tortured you and shows no sign of remorse, no flicker of regret, sorrow or repentance?

Torture happens for a variety of reasons. Sometimes it is 'justified' by the desire to extract information, the so-called 'ticking bomb' argument – if you can extract information from a terrorist quickly enough you can save people from a planned atrocity. It is also used as a way to terrorize groups or populations and to reinforce oppression or stifle opposition. Torture has been deployed as a form of extreme punishment for prisoners. But torture does not only happen because there is a rationale for it, however perverse. One of the more shocking aspects of the murder of the boy, whose mother I mentioned in Chapter 1, is that it emerged in the trial of his killers that he was tortured in the days before he was strangled. The details of that were literally sickening but the more chilling thought was that there seemed to be no obvious motive.

Sometimes, perhaps often, torture happens because a cruel person finds themselves in a position of power over someone else and they decide to use it, and exploit the other for their own pleasure and enjoyment. Or rather, they don't so much decide as fail to resist the temptation to exploit their power. The film version of *Death and the Maiden* ends differently to the play, and in it the torturer's final confession makes just this point: I *could* do it. So I *did*.

Torture takes many forms but can be defined as the intentional and humiliating infliction of excruciating pain. In some cases the focus is on causing extreme physical pain. In other cases the point is to induce fear by a number of means so that the infliction of humiliation and the sense of being dominated and without personal worth or dignity predominate. In both cases, physical and psychological pain are deployed to break down the victim and undermine their identity. Both are real but the psychological damage can last years and decades longer than the physical. It can dominate a person's experience for the rest of their life.

Elaine Scarry who has written about pain and torture, argues that the pain can be literally beyond language, reducing the sufferer to a pre-linguistic state. Victim of torture, Jacobo Timerman, has testified from his own experience: 'When electric shocks are applied, all that a man feels is that they are ripping apart his flesh. And he howls.'[3] When the torture is politically motivated the victim is deliberately robbed of his or her own voice. According to Scarry, the impact of physical pain on the psyche is integral to this. It not only demands attention but insists on full attention. People speak of 'blinding pain' because it removes all other perception and indeed consciousness, 'the enormity of the agony is the sufferer's only reality'.[4] All sense of past and future, and therefore continuity and identity, are lost. Time is collapsed into the present moment and yet the experience persists beyond the time of actual inflicted torture. As Sheila Cassidy, herself a victim of torture, puts it:

> In between questioning sessions I lay huddled on the bed under the blanket, numb and unseeing. It was as though I was suspended over a pit: the past had no relevance and I could see no future. I lived only for the minute that was and in the fear of further pain.[5]

William Cavanaugh, who engages theologically with the reality of torture in his book *Torture and Eucharist*, emphasizes that torture breaks down community and creates what he calls 'individuals'. Such a way of putting it can be easily misunderstood. But he is not thinking of the individual as an integrated and wholesome person of dignity but as someone – almost *something* – cut off from all forms of social connectedness and meaning: someone radically isolated, who has been robbed not only of their own self but also of their own voice.

> Psychologists who work with torture victims point to the destruction of the victim as political actor through the fragmentation of the ego. The feeling and reality of powerlessness in torture is so extreme that the subject is no longer subject, but mere object. The ego is dissolved because it cannot sustain the processes necessary for self-preservation. In fact, death, the very negation of ego, becomes desirable.[6]

Certainly there are plenty of stories of people who have been tortured committing suicide and many more speak of it, desire it and try it. The aim of torture is to destroy personhood and personal freedom. To the degree that it is successful it makes forgiveness literally impossible because only a person of freedom can engage in forgiveness. However, there are stories of the aftermath of torture which are understood as forgiveness stories. One of the more famous is that of Eric Lomax, a prisoner of war in the Far East in the Second World War.

## The Railway Man

Eric Lomax wrote up his experiences in the book *The Railway Man*. After publication, it quickly became well known as a book 'about forgiveness'. And yet the question of forgiveness does not arise until very near the end. In the twenty first century, forgiveness is much closer to the public mind than it was in the years that followed the Second World War. Lomax's book, published in 1996, it reflects a wave of new interest in forgiveness but is not a book which suggests that forgiveness is quick or easy. Nor is it a forgiveness story in the naïve sense that suggests that Lomax identified 'forgiveness' as something he would aim to achieve in the immediate aftermath of either his first beating or his subsequent torture. Even much later, in 1987, his view was that he would rather cut his right arm off than engage in correspondence with a repentant Japanese ex-soldier.[7]

As well as writing about his experiences in various Japanese POW jails, Lomax tells the reader something about how difficult he himself was to live with in the years after the war. This comes across more clearly in the belief account on the Forgiveness Project website[8], presumably written some years after the book, but is also evident in the way in which he describes his (understandable) intolerance with the pettiness of small-town and chapel life in the post-war years.[9] Underlying this, however, is a deeper and more important narrative which is initiated when he begins to receive support from the Medical Foundation for the Care of Victims of Torture (Medical Foundation). The starting point of the *forgiveness* story is when people begin to listen to him as he talks about his physical experiences and, more significantly, about their continued psychological impact on him.

Lomax writes movingly of his experience of being welcomed on his first visit to the Medical Foundation by Helen Bamber: 'She was utterly unhurried… She seemed to have infinite time, endless patience and sympathy; but above all she gave me time. It was astonishing simply to know that the pressure of everyday life would not drown out what I had to say.'[10] For Lomax, the meeting was like 'walking through a door into an unexplored world, a world of caring and special understanding'.[11] But it was not only Bamber who listened: 'I was amazed again and again that everyone at the Foundation from the Director to the newest and youngest member of staff cared enough to observe and listen, and to listen again. I could hardly believe that I was beginning to talk.'[12]

What is especially significant about this, I suggest, is that for the first time Lomax had the experience of being in the company of those who would share his memories and simply be with him as he let himself recall and talk about what had happened to him; as he rediscovered his voice. This 'being with' was characterized by a degree of empathy and acceptance in the listening and that in turn allowed Lomax to reveal to himself the impact that the experience of torture was continuing to have on his personality and character. It becomes clear that being listened to in 'guided conversations' every four weeks for two years had a profound effect on his self-awareness:

> I was aware of myself for the first time as a person for whom the idea of torture might hold some answers – why I was such a strange combination of stubbornness, passivity and silent hostility; why I was unable to express open anger, and why I found authority so difficult; and why I was sometimes unable to feel.[13]

It was after two years of this kind of care that Lomax came across an article written by a man called Nagase Takashi. As he read the article, he experienced what he called 'a strange, icy joy of the weirdest kind'. He recognized the face of the elderly man in the photograph and knew that this was the interpreter who had been present when he was subjected to what Lomax calls 'the historic water torture' but which is today known as 'waterboarding'. That word does not begin to do justice to Lomax's experience. Writing in the *The Times* in 2008, however, he summarized its horror:

> I was laid on my back on a bench; my arms, still broken and almost useless, were placed across my chest; my face was covered by a cloth and a tap feeding a hose-pipe was turned on. It was all so simple. To encourage me to say something the senior Japanese man beat me from time to time with the branch of a tree. This did not do my arms any good at all. The interpreter, who did not seem sympathetic to the whole procedure, held my left hand. I suspected that he wanted to make sure that I remained alive.[14]

Lomax says that of all the people who had been involved in his ill-treatment, abuse and torture, this translator was the only one he remembered with a voice and a face. It was clear from his article that this man had himself suffered with nightmares and flashbacks since that time. It also said that he had been seriously involved in charitable work and in finding ways to ensure that the many POWs who had died under the Japanese were remembered and memorialized. Lomax admits a moment of 'vengeful glory' here, delighting that he was not the only one to continue to suffer. But he also registered a degree of connection when he wrote: 'This strange man was obviously drawn on in his work by memories of my own cries of distress and fear.'[15]

The seriousness of the suffering that Lomax experienced should not be underestimated:

> The whole operation was a long and agonising sequence of near-drowning, choking, vomiting and muscular struggling

> with the water flowing with ever-changing force. To put it mildly, it was ghastly, quite the worst experience of my life. There were occasional intervals for interrogation. How long the torture lasted, I do not know. It covered a period of some days, with periods of unconsciousness and semi-consciousness. Eventually I was dumped in my cell, which was so small it offered little scope for movement. At about this time two of my colleagues were beaten to death. Their bodies were dumped in a latrine where they may well remain to this day.[16]

Taken together, the memory of the suffering and the new knowledge of the attitude and behaviour of the interpreter, were difficult for Lomax to handle and he took some time to work out his response. Before long, however, he decided that he wanted to meet Nagase. Not that forgiveness was on his mind. Rather it was his intention to see whether his expressions of remorse were genuine. It seemed that Nagase had repented. But was it real and sincere? Did his repentance in some sense meet the reality of the suffering? At this time, some people began to suggest to him it was time to forgive and forget. 'I don't normally argue openly about anything,' he writes, 'but I began to argue just a little about this. The majority of people who hand out advice about forgiveness have not gone through the sort of experience I had; I was not inclined to forgive, not yet, and probably never.'[17] In fact, his thoughts were far from forgiving, 'I still thought often about striking him down, but Stuart (from the Medical Foundation) helped me to see beyond murder.'[18]

The next idea to formulate itself in his mind was to arrange to meet Nagase but not to reveal in advance his identity as the prisoner who had been tortured for making and keeping a map. The plan was to spring this information on him during the encounter, preferably in front of television cameras. That did not come to pass, however, and in the meanwhile a Japanese professor of history visited Lomax to seek help with her research on the 'romusha'.[19] This encounter began to create in Lomax a different kind of regard for Japan and therefore the Japanese. The possibility that Nagase was more than a torturer, and Japanese people more than wantonly cruel, began to become real to him.

Shortly after that, he came across a seventy-page autobiography written by Nagase called *Crosses and Tigers*. Reading the book, he is struck by the way in which the conscripted Nagase writes about his first impressions of the POW camps. It is clear that he sees with an eye of compassion and is an anguished soul caught between the duties of obedience and a degree of empathy with the suffering prisoners. This agony is exacerbated when it comes to describing the torture of Lomax himself:

> Watching the prisoner in great torture, I almost lost my presence of mind. I was desperate to control my shaking body. I feared that he would be killed in my presence… With the prisoner screaming and crying 'Mother!' Mother!' I muttered to myself, 'Mother, do you know what is happening to your son now?' I still cannot stop shuddering every time I recall that horrible scene.[20]

One particular aspect of the small book is deeply curious. Nagase describes an occasion when he visits a large war cemetery in Kanburi. He offers a wreath at the base of a white cross in the middle of the 7,000 graves and he prays. He writes: 'I felt my body emitting yellow beams of light in every direction and turning transparent. At that moment, I thought: "This is it. You have been pardoned."'[21]

Lomax read all this with some detachment but wondered about Nagase's feeling of having been forgiven. 'God may have forgiven him, but I had not; mere human forgiveness is another matter.'[22] His wife, however, found it very provocative. So she wrote to Nagase suggesting that it would be good for the two men to meet but added: 'How can you feel 'forgiven' Mr Nagase, if this particular former Far Eastern prisoner-of-war has not yet forgiven you?' [23] Nagase wrote back saying that these words have 'beaten me down wholely, reminding me of my dirty old days,' and he adds at the very end of the letter, 'the dagger of your letter thrusted me into my heart to the bottom.'[24]

The effect of the reply was startling. His wife found it beautiful and her anger drained away. Lomax writes of his own response:

> In that moment I lost whatever hard armour I had wrapped around me and began to think the unthinkable: that I could meet Nagase face to face in simple good will. Forgiveness became more than an abstract idea: it was now a real possibility.[25]

This is an immensely significant moment. It has three aspects: the dropping of well established defences, the liberation of the imagination (thinking the unthinkable) and the emerging possibility that forgiveness might be real rather than abstract. It is a time of release and discovery, healing and reintegration. Lomax was beginning to become a new person. But the new person was not something of his own creation. This was no 'make-over' of his character. Rather, it was the moment when the possibility of integrating his memory of suffering in the past with the desire to take responsibility for making this better in the future came together. Out of this fusion came the capacity and desire to think and say whatever might be necessary to connect these two in the present.

A year later the two men met in Kanburi near the River Kwae Bridge. Although Lomax felt that David Lean's film had made it 'too famous' ('who has ever seen such well-fed POWs?') it was here that Nagase had been responsible for building a Buddhist chapel of reconciliation.

Lomax describes their meeting. Nagase is overcome with emotion and so Lomax's capacity for reserve and self-control comes into its own: '[it] helped me to help him.'[26] Nagase initially cannot say much more than 'I am very, very sorry,' but goes on to say: 'I never forgot you, I remember your face, especially your eyes.' Then, Lomax records:

> He asked if he could touch my hand. My former interrogator held my arm, which was so much larger than his, stroking it quite unselfconsciously. I don't find it embarrassing. He gripped my wrist with both hands and told me that when I was being tortured – he used the word – he measured my pulse. I remembered he had written this in his memoir. Yet now that we were face to face, his grief seemed more acute than mine. 'I was a member of the Japanese Imperial Army, we treated your countrymen very, very, badly,' he said. 'We both survived,' I said encouragingly, really believing it now.[27]

It would be possible for the story to end there, and yet Lomax felt that it was wrong to assume that the question of forgiveness had been adequately resolved. 'I felt I had to respond to Nagase's sense of the binding or loosening force of my decision.'[28] It is interesting and significant that in this phase of the process Lomax was led by Nagase's needs. Someone explained to him how in Buddhist thought unforgiven evil acts like this would be returned to the soul in another life. Although not fully understanding the theology, Lomax wanted to free Nagase from any further suffering and the only question remaining was how to offer forgiveness with appropriate formality.

The opportunity came when they were in Japan. All this time the two men had never been alone together. When Lomax asked to be alone with him Nagase was afraid and his wife too was concerned and simply said, 'Heart', as a reminder of his frail condition and vulnerability. Once alone, Lomax read out a letter he had written which, after asserting that the war had ended fifty years previously, noted Nagase's own suffering, his work for reconciliation and his courageous stance against militarism. He concluded: 'I told him that while I could not forget what happened in Kanburi in 1943, I assured him of my total forgiveness.'[29] Nagase was again overcome with emotion.

## Reflection

The most obvious point about Lomax's forgiveness story is that it took a very long time. The forgiving took place half a century after the event. The second point is that, as far as we can tell, very little happened in the first forty years of that time. It was only after Lomax was cared for and listened to by the Medical Foundation that the process of healing could begin. There was a loosening and a discovery of personal freedom. Through healing he began to recover himself. He tells us very little about what he experienced as he began to find the words to describe his experiences and his feelings. He does tell us, however, that the mental and emotional scars are deeper than the physical wounds. He also tells us about his growth in self-awareness and the way in which the visit of a Japanese professor happened to coincide with his increasing openness and that it encouraged him to develop an interest and a curiosity in an area of life that was blanked off to him by his trauma.

But if length of time is the most obvious factor in this story, the apparent accidents of timing are, if anything, more significant. The order in which things happened allowed Lomax's story to develop into a forgiveness story. We have already noted that he did not intend it to be any such thing for most of that half century. When he first read *Crosses and Tigers* he was not himself ready to engage emotionally with it. It was his wife's letter, and she was his second wife, which conveyed the anger that predicated a new depth of sadness in Nagase. The turning point came when she communicated this in her reply.

Other factors beyond Lomax's control were also of immense importance: the personality of Nagase, for instance. Not every such interpreter would have been as sensitive to the victim's suffering, few would have lived out their regret and remorse in positive good works and very few would have written a book about it. Even if they had, the chances of it falling into the hands of the man with the map are not that high. Furthermore, few would have been able to allow themselves to be moved to deeper levels of heartbreak (as he expressed in response to Mrs Lomax's angry letter, for instance) and then expressions of repentance. All this leads me to conclude, without intending any disrespect for the part that Lomax himself played, that it is not so much that Lomax wrote a story of forgiveness with his life, rather, it was that Lomax found himself within a forgiveness story.

The implications of this conclusion for the way we read the story are quite important. It becomes clear, when put like this, that Lomax did not in any sense intend or achieve forgiveness. It was something that happened because he played his part as a complex and uncertain plot unfolded. He did so with great dignity, integrity and, in the end, generosity and good will. But the point that is vital here is that the plot of this forgiveness story was not driven by the will of the main character. While this is of some importance in the way we read the story, it is of massive importance for the way in which we draw implications and imperatives for other people who are victims of serious harm or violation.

The point is simply this. Whether or not you can forgive is not all down to you. Your role is to play your part in the story that unfolds with honesty, integrity, generosity and courage. Indeed, having read this story I am inclined to conclude that it might be *unhelpful* to think that there is a virtue called 'forgivingness' and that there are some people who have it, while others who do not, even allowing for the nuance of infinitely varying degrees.[30] There are only events and responses and a small number of virtues which might or might not be brought into play depending on a variety of contingencies. This *is* a forgiveness story, but it might not have been. Forgiveness stories are wonderful but they do not happen simply because a person, who is seriously and unjustly harmed, lets go of their resentment or accepts an apology. Forgiveness is something much stranger than that and more vulnerable to matters outside the victim's control.

Reflecting further on Lomax's story we see the way in which, although forgiveness was once impossible and unimaginable for him, he was gradually drawn into a situation where it became a realistic and meaningful possibility. But this would not have happened without the healing which was achieved through the care he received from the Medical Foundation or the way in which this led to a wider interest in things Japanese, which in turn led to coming across Nagase's book and ultimately meeting him. It is also clear that for some reason Lomax and Nagase were able to form a bond through relating together. Releasing Nagase from the consequences of his evil actions in the past was another distinct step and this was in part, it seems, a response to Nagase's extensive atoning work.

This is a story with several distinct threads, which, from time to time, connect and tie up. This multithreaded quality is integral to the conclusion that it really can be called *a forgiveness story*. It is remarkable both because so many of the strands actually existed and because of the combination of care, character and serendipity which between them, formed a context or environment in which forgiveness became both desirable and possible. It is indeed a wonderful story. But if we take it as *ideal* forgiveness story then we risk making life extremely difficult for others, both victims and offenders, who are caught up in stories with fewer of the threads that make forgiveness possible.

## The Sunflower

In the famous book, *The Sunflower*, Simon Wiesenthal describes the occasion when, as an inmate in a concentration camp, he was called to the bedside of a dying SS Officer who wanted to confess his part in a terrible atrocity – and receive forgiveness. After hearing what he had to say, Wiesenthal remained silent and left the room. On returning to the camp he discussed the event with his friends. Was he right to remain silent? Adam and Arthur rebuked him for even asking: there is one more dead Nazi, that is all there is to say. Josek said that Wiesenthal did the right thing but is wrong to agonize about it. He had no forgiveness to offer as he was not himself one who had suffered at the man's hands. He adds that if the SS man had wanted absolution he should have sent for a Christian priest. Two years later a Polish seminarian replaced a dead cohabitant of Wiesenthal's bunk. His opinion was also solicited. He felt that Wiesenthal did the man a service simply by listening to him but was mean-spirited not to have responded in a positive way to his repentance.

After the war Wiesenthal wrote his story and circulated it to thirty-six different public figures asking for their response. The story and the responses were published in *The Sunflower: A Symposium.*[31] The title is often overlooked in discussions, but it contains a vital clue as to why this is not a story of forgiveness. Whereas it was likely that Wiesenthal's corpse would soon lie in an unmarked mass grave, the SS Officer's would lie in a cemetery with a sunflower sprouting from the earth over his feet. The degrading anonymity is reinforced when the SS Officer said to Wiesenthal as he was begging forgiveness: 'I do not know who you are, I only know that you are Jew and that is enough.'[32]

The symposium inevitably revealed a wide range of ways of looking at this situation and responding to it. The situation can be eased a little if we distinguish between forgiveness and pardon, as mentioned earlier.[33] The SS man wanted to be absolved, and absolution is a form of pardon. That is why it did not matter to him who Wiesenthal was. He wanted an authority figure to say something to relieve him of the guilt he was feeling and which he believed he was going to carry to his judgement beyond the grave. He knew enough, however, to appreciate that it would be neither sensible nor possible to summon a priest to his bedside when he was surrounded by so many people, all of whom were in an indirect way his victims or, as he looked at it, 'representatives' of the people whom he had harmed and killed. It was a crass mistake to make, looking for a formula to deliver forgiveness in the context of a concentration camp, but it is nonetheless possible to understand the confusion that allowed him to make it. The officer felt that he was doing something more honourable by turning to someone whose voice might have been the voice of the victim than turning to a priest who could be relied upon to proffer death-bed absolution when presented with contrition. Yet the irony in the request is all too apparent in the way in which he dismisses any question of Wiesenthal's personal identity, thereby reinforcing one of the attitudes on which the Nazi regime in general, and extermination and labour camps in particular, were based.

Reading this story in the light of *The Railway Man*, which was not published until long after Wiesenthal had conducted his symposium, is of great help in making these clarifications. The SS man obviously had troubling feelings about the massacre that he was involved in. But what is any observer to make of these feelings? One thing that became clear in *The Railway Man* is that it took Lomax a very long time to work out what to make of the various projects and communications which flowed from Nagase after the war.

His capacity to come to a sympathetic understanding of these also depended on many other events and interactions. These were all much more substantial than the death-bed expression of regret which Wiesenthal witnessed. For forgiveness to have substance in this context, it would need to be more than an obliging response to a request to be forgiven which is freighted with regret and remorse. It is simply not enough to regret one particular atrocity, the images of which haunt your waking and sleeping hours, in the context of ongoing oppressive violence. In such a situation the potential forgiver does not have enough space in which to work. It is as if a kidnapper were to ask forgiveness for a beating that he inflicted on a captive without raising the question of setting the captive free.

What the SS man wanted from Wiesenthal was the equivalent of the exchange that eventually happened when Lomax read a formal letter to Nagase. Lomax makes it clear in his book that he was not entirely sure why this was necessary and that he did not really understand the Buddhist 'theology' which made it so. However, he went through with it in a very serious way. It happened when the two were alone, and it is intriguing that Lomax did not explain why. Nor did he disclose the full contents of the letter in his book. We are in strange territory here, where important boundaries exist but also overlap. This is a private matter – and yet it is the subject of a book. From Lomax's end it is forgiveness but from Nagase's end it is experienced as both forgiveness and pardon.

All this is possible – both the ambiguity and the clarity, both the enigma and the formal closure – because of the length and the nature of the process that had led up to the formal meeting. Wiesenthal, on the other hand, was called into a situation cold, still wearing the prison pyjamas that were the sign of his unfreedom, and asked to do at least two impossible things: to pardon and to forgive. Pardon can only be given by an authority figure and Wiesenthal had no authority. The SS man tried to invest him with some by saying 'you are Jew' but this only revealed how muddled he was. No Jew would feel authorized to offer pardon after a massacre 'as a Jew'.

Apart from theological issues this exacerbates the underlying offence which is the denial of humanity and individuality: the treating of people as things. No human being would feel that there was a basis for interpersonal forgiveness in such a brief encounter. The tragedy is that he was so alienated from the concept of justice that he could not see that the way in which he tried to seek pardon made forgiveness not only unlikely, but impossible. Forgiveness is difficult to pin down but it is always a gift freely given by a person who is given respect by the person who is forgiven. Without this recognition of personal freedom, without the respect, there can be no forgiveness because the victim has not got anything to give or withhold. Only the free can forgive. (Yet it is only those who are not yet free who have something to forgive.)

Wiesenthal could, of course, have play-acted. He could have intuited what the man wanted and gone through the motions. He could even have believed himself to have forgiven the man. But I don't think that either of these things could have changed the plot of this story to make it into a forgiveness story. The vital point here is that forgiveness is not always possible after unjust harm has been inflicted. It needs the conditions, the environment, the ecology of relationships and attention to the consequences of the harm and the demands of justice. Forgiveness is only sometimes a possibility between human beings. There are occasions when it is not possible. It cannot just be pulled out of a hat like a magician's rabbit.

Many of the Christian participants in the symposium wanted to see more evidence of a forgiving spirit from Wiesenthal. My feeling is that they projected themselves into this situation and wrote the story up in such a way as to reinforce their self-ideal as compassionate and kind. I have great sympathy with this and no objection to it until it begins to be framed as if it were full forgiveness or a duty for others. Justice requires both that forgiveness lies in the gift of the victim and that it comes from his or her heart and that pardon is only given on objective grounds by an authority figure acting in role.

Compassion, has a different dynamic and brings different demands than does justice. It requires that the person who is spoken to in some way reaches out empathically to the other, in this case a remorseful and frightened man on his deathbed. It is a very sad aspect of this story that by summoning the prisoner and by asking for forgiveness, the SS man actually constricts the space for both compassion and empathy. The gulf between Wiesenthal's life and that of the officer, symbolized by the sunflower, is enormous, and Wiesenthal is being invited, or required, to bridge that gulf entirely from his own side.

Put like this, the difficulty becomes apparent. If there is to be any empathy here, it is to be unidirectional. The SS man has shown that empathy is beyond him. All he knows is the exercise of power. Once again it is clear that work and effort are being demanded of the one who is not free to do the work. All Wiesenthal can do is assert his freedom by *not* responding as required. He has to walk away silently in order to assert his dignity and protect his spiritual freedom. And he *has* to protect them, otherwise he falls into the trap of unfreedom which is where the dying SS officer tragically finds himself. That Wiesenthal does walk away silently is an act of courage and dignity.

The irony here is that the SS man could only be freed from his torment, only be 'forgiven' by Wiesenthal, if he had in some way recognized his humanity and seen the tragedy of its denial in this context. As the SS Officer expressed no empathic understanding, Wiesenthal could not begin to forgive him. It is precisely this entering into the world and mind and heart of the other which allows the possibility of mutual identification and some kind of relationship which is necessary for forgiveness.

In *The Railway Man* this is exactly what happened. Lomax was able to forgive both because Nagase empathized with his suffering personally and because he (Lomax) was able to recover his own wholeness and integrity through a number of factors, not least the care and attention he received from Helen Bamber and her colleagues at the Medical Foundation. That this process took the best part of fifty years is also relevant. Wisesenthal was expected to respond instantly.

My conclusion is that *The Sunflower* is very much *not* a forgiveness story. Rather it is a story of spiritual torment. Set within an environment of dehumanizing imprisonment, the request to forgive is excruciating and cruel. The SS man was unwittingly, but nonetheless actually, tormenting Wiesenthal with some of the higher delights that human beings enjoy and in which they can find their dignity and esteem: offering forgiveness and mercy, and reaching out with empathy and compassion. Having dominated the prisoner's body this was an attempt to dominate yet further his voice and his feelings, his soul. But Wiesenthal walked away silently. He did the right thing. His freedom had been taken. His voice had been denied. He had been given a script but declined to play the part. He would have had to have been a superhuman to have found a way of responding which conveyed kindness while remaining truthful about the evil of the situation. He carried the torment with him from the camp partly because the episode told him that here was a situation in which his truest human voice was called for and yet denied at the same time.

In the years after the war, Wiesenthal attempted to recover the voice of the victim and pursue justice. The story of *The Sunflower* goes on to tell us how he sought out the mother of this SS Officer and established some broader, richer and more sympathetic sense of him as a person. We cannot tell what might have happened in that relationship had the officer lived. Read carefully, however, *The Sunflower* has a great deal to tell us about the limits of forgiveness, and the difficulty and anguish involved when any person is treated as an object or non-person by another. By writing the story Wiesenthal perhaps recovered the voice that was silent as he left the man's bedside. In inviting others to join in the symposium he facilitated a wider ethical and spiritual conversation. One way in which to promote forgiveness now is to seek to develop that conversation with the benefit of both hindsight and the appreciation that impossible situations emerge all the time. One aspect of that conversation will always be: 'What do you say about forgiveness when talking about forgiveness is impossible or unwise?' It is a vital question for those who seek to be good companions to victims to keep alive.

## Notes

1. Dorfman, A. *Death and Maiden*, p. 34.
2. Dorfman, A. *Death and Maiden*, p. 35.
3. Cavanaugh, W. *Torture and Eucharist*, p. 35.
4. Cavanaugh, W. *Torture and Eucharist*, p. 37.
5. Cassidy, S. *Audacity to Believe*, p. 198.
6. Cavanaugh, W. *Torture and Eucharist*, p. 40.
7. Lomax, E. *The Railway Man*, p. 232.
8. http://theforgivenessproject.com/stories/eric-lomax-scotland/.
9. One of the intriguing silences in *The Railway Man* concerns the relationship that Lomax did or did not make between his faith and his experience and its effect on him.
10. Lomax, E. *The Railway Man*, p. 235.
11. Lomax, E. *The Railway Man*, p. 236.
12. Lomax, E. *The Railway Man*, p. 237.
13. Lomax, E. *The Railway Man*, p. 237.
14. Lomax, E. 'Waterboarding: The Most Horrific Experience of My Life', *The Times*, 4 March 2008.
15. Lomax, E. *The Railway Man*, p. 240.
16. Lomax, E. 'Waterboarding: The Most Horrific Experience of My Life', *The Times*, 4 March 2008.

17. Lomax, E. *The Railway Man*, p. 241.
18. Lomax, E. *The Railway Man*, p. 242.
19. The quarter of a million people of various races and language groups who were labourers on the railway but whose story was still unwritten and unknown. Lomax, E. *The Railway Man*, p. 244.
20. Lomax, E. *The Railway Man*, pp. 248–249.
21. Lomax, E. *The Railway Man*, p. 251.
22. Lomax, E. *The Railway Man*, p. 252.
23. Lomax, E. *The Railway Man*, p. 253.
24. Lomax, E. *The Railway Man*, p. 255.
25. Lomax, E. *The Railway Man*, p. 255.
26. Lomax, E. *The Railway Man*, p. 263.
27. Lomax, E. *The Railway Man*, p. 264.
28. Lomax, E. *The Railway Man*, p. 269.
29. Lomax, E. *The Railway Man*, p. 275.
30. An extensive exploration of the virtue of forgivingness is found in an article by Robert C. Roberts called 'Forgivingness' in *American Philosophical Quarterly* 32, 1995: pp. 289–306.
31. Wiesenthal, S. *The Sunflower*.
32. Wiesenthal, S. *The Sunflower*, p. 54.
33. See above, pp. 7–8

CHAPTER 4

# A Duty to Forgive?

In October 2006 a terrible atrocity happened at Nickel Mines, Pennsylvania. Five schoolgirls were shot and another five wounded by a local man who had imprisoned them in their school room. Before he could be arrested he shot himself. The response of the Amish community to which they belonged was remarkable. Without any coordination, members set about trying to console and help not only the families of the victims but also the family of the gunman. They also set about expressing forgiveness to that family and extending it to the gunman himself. In a lovely book about this called *Amish Grace*, the theology of the community comes across through interviews. An elder explained emphatically:

> Forgiveness is the only thing that Jesus underscored in the Lord's Prayer. Do you know that Jesus speaks about forgiveness in the two verses right after the Lord's Prayer? So you see, it's really central to the Lord's Prayer. It's really intense.[1]

Those two verses read: 'For if you forgive others their trespasses, your heavenly Father will also forgive you; but if you do not forgive others, neither will your Father forgive your trespasses' (Matthew 6.14 & 15). When the playwright and theologian

Charles Williams wrote a book about forgiveness he focused on that little word 'as' found in the prayer itself 'forgive us our trespasses *as* we forgive those who trespass against us'. He took a view which was very like that of the Amish: 'No other word in English carries a greater possibility of terror than that little word 'as' in that clause...'[2] There is threat here: forgive or else! 'Forgiveness of injuries is demanded of the Christian because of the nature of our Lord, and it is demanded entirely.'[3] In this chapter we explore whether the New Testament's teaching on forgiveness really is as simple and as stark as this. Is there a straightforward duty and obligation on Christian people always to forgive?

Forgiveness certainly has a high profile in the New Testament. We see it in the first miracle in Mark's gospel, the healing of the paralytic (Mark 2). We learn about it in the parables and stories in Luke's gospel, the prodigal son (Luke 15) and the story of the woman in the house of Simon (Luke 7) and of Zacchaeus (Luke 19). We are warned that we will be judged by our willingness to forgive in Matthew's gospel in the story of the unforgiving steward (Matthew 18). We hear words of forgiveness not only from the lips of the dying Jesus (Luke 23.34) but also from Stephen, the first martyr (Acts 7.60).[4]

Paul expects forgiveness to feature in the life and ethos of the churches. Writing to the Colossians he states:

> As God's chosen ones, holy and beloved, clothe yourselves with compassion, kindness, humility, meekness, and patience. Bear with one another and, if anyone has a complaint against another, forgive each other; just as the Lord has forgiven you, so you also must forgive. (Colossians 3.12-13)[5]

Similar words are found in the letter to the Ephesians:

> Put away from you all bitterness and wrath and anger and wrangling and slander, together with all malice, and be kind to one another, tender-hearted, forgiving one another, as God in Christ has forgiven you. (Ephesians 4.31-32)

In Chapter 18 of Matthew's gospel, Peter asks how many times he should forgive and is told, 'not seven times, but, I tell you, seventy-seven times.' (Matthew 18.22). This brief conversation with Peter is followed by the parable of the servant who fails to forgive an underling a minor debt, despite the fact that he has been forgiven a massive debt. When the Lord hears about this he is extremely angry and hands the servant over to be tortured 'until he should pay his entire debt.' (Matthew 18.34). Just to make sure that the people get the message Jesus adds, 'So my heavenly Father will also do to every one of you, if you do not forgive your brother or sister from your heart' (Matthew 18.35). A similar message is heard in Mark's gospel when Jesus says, 'Whenever you stand praying, forgive, if you have anything against anyone; so that your Father in heaven may also forgive you your trespasses' (Mark 11.25).

As the elder from Nickel Mines reminded us, the imperative to forgive is also found at the heart of the prayer that Jesus teaches his disciples when they ask him how to pray. Luke's version puts it like this: 'And forgive us our sins, for we ourselves forgive everyone indebted to us.' (Luke 11.4). As we have seen, Matthew not only makes the same point but adds words after the prayer to underline it (Matthew 6.14 & 15).

The message of these passages seems to be that we are forgiven to the extent to which we forgive others. It is strong medicine, to be sure. But we should not think of it as poison. Jesus does not want us to try to do anything that is impossible. In particular, Jesus does not want us to confuse who we are with who God is. One danger with these passages is that they can be read as suggesting that human beings forgive in much the same way that God forgives. But God's forgiveness and human forgiveness are very different things. They are connected, like members of a family, but nonetheless different. Any interpretation of the challenge represented in these passages must take that into account. They cannot mean: 'you must forgive in the same way that God forgives', because that is impossible.[6] What they can mean, however, is that you must set about forgiving others as part and parcel of the process of seeking the forgiveness of God.

Tom Wright suggests that this all needs to be understood in terms of what he calls the 'human logic of forgiveness'. Writing specifically about Matthew 18 he comments that:

> Jesus is not giving a kind of arbitrary, abstract commandment and then saying that if you fail to meet the test God will not forgive you… He is drawing attention to a fact about the moral universe and human nature. He is telling us, in effect, that the faculty we have for receiving forgiveness and the faculty we have for granting forgiveness are one and the same thing. If we open the one, we shall open the other. If we slam the door on the one, we slam the door on the other.[7]

Wright's comment moves us away from the ethics of forgiveness to its spirituality. Anthony Bash does something similar in his discussion of Mark 11.25, suggesting that the point is not so much that God withholds forgiveness from those who do not forgive but that those who do not forgive are unable to receive forgiveness.[8] I think this shift is helpful and appropriate and that it suggests a very helpful insight into the nature of forgiveness. Like prayer, it is matter of spirituality rather than simple duty. Praying and forgiving are ongoing aspects of a wholesome life.

The passage from Colossians is not precisely about prayer but it is about the distinctive set of attitudes that the disciple must adopt: 'compassion, kindness, humility, meekness and patience'. It is such attitudes and virtues which are primary, whereas the action of forgiving is a consequence and outworking of them.

The passage from the letter to the Ephesians, while rightly connecting forgiveness with the determination to be rid of wrath and bitterness and so on, is perhaps not translated as clearly as it might be when it says 'forgiving one another as God in Christ has forgiven you'. One only has to replace the word 'as' with 'since' however, to move the sense from the ethics and psychology of forgiveness to the spirituality of forgiveness. Christians are to forgive others *since* and because God in Christ has forgiven them. But the forgiving that they do is both similar to *and* different from the forgiving that they receive.

The most challenging and stark of the 'duty to forgive' passages is Matthew 18. Is this really about the spirituality of forgiving, about having a forgiving disposition and attitude, rather than being a determined and complete forgiver of others, 'come what may'? I think it is. As with all biblical interpretation, the immediate context is of great importance in helping us get the appropriate message from pithy words and phrases. The context here is the amazing story of the slave who is let off an enormous debt and then fails to let a fellow slave off a minor debt. The story is plainly about the way in which mercy works in God's economy: 'should you not have had mercy on your fellow-slave, as I had mercy on you?' (Matthew 18.33). The question is rhetorical because Jesus' teaching about the love, grace or mercy of God is always the same. It is not a reward or benefit for an individual to enjoy but a healing delight which comes to full fruition when it is passed on to others.

The wider context of the story is Peter's question about how often he should forgive, 'if another member of the church sins against me' (Matthew 18.21). The answer of seventy-seven times is intended to undermine the terms on which the question is set; to shift it from the quantitative to the qualitative. It does not mean that you must forgive very many times but that you must be a forgiving person at heart.

It is vital to be clear about this if we are to understand the social and ethical implication of what Jesus teaches about forgiveness. There is no road to the kingdom of God which does not involve forgiveness of others. But this is because of the larger point that the orientation required of us to participate in God's kingdom is one of love: love of God, love of self, love of neighbours and love of enemies. That love will take different forms in different relationships. (The injunction to love yourself does not mean to indulge yourself or flatter your own ego… ) It will form our character and personality, our dispositions and attitudes, in different ways so that we develop those distinctively Christian virtues of compassion, kindness and so on. The question of whether a Christian should 'forgive' under certain circumstances is not an easy one to deal with. It certainly does not instantly admit the answer, 'yes, of course, see Matthew 18'. The question which *does* have a simple answer is: 'Should a Christian have a forgiving heart?' and the answer to that is 'absolutely, yes'.

The problem that we have, the problem that this book seeks to clarify and wrestle with is: 'What does a person with a forgiving heart do when they find themselves in a situation where it seems not only difficult, but impossible, unimaginable or even wrong to forgive?' The question of forgiveness posed here is essentially the question of how we love those who have unjustly hurt us. The answer to this question cannot be taken in isolation from questions which surround it. We cannot find an easy answer to the question of how we love those who have hurt us anymore than we can find an easy answer to the question of how we love God, how we love our self, how we love each particular neighbour, and so on.

To answer any of these questions adequately takes time and warrants careful and deep, prayerful and spiritual, consideration. Moreover, it rarely results in a thought or theory of what to do which we then implement or apply. Rather it issues in attitudes of mind, the way we spend our time, the kind of regard we give people and in numerous small actions. In short, it involves our dispositions of heart. This is the way we 'love' as human beings and I see no reason to suppose that we forgive in ways that are less subtle and sophisticated.

What is abundantly clear from this analysis is that Jesus teaching about the duty to forgive *does not* mean that we have to throw away all our moral scruples and concern with justice and say 'well, I forgive you because it matters more to me that God forgives me than that I continue to hold you to account'. What it *does* mean is that we cannot persist in our transformative pilgrimage to becoming participants in the kingdom of God while wilfully dividing up hearts so that this bit is open to forgiveness and that bit closed off to the same dynamic. Nor does it mean that we can follow Jesus and at the same time actively seek to stockpile resentment, hatred and bitterness against those who have harmed us.

When we are victims of unjust hurt or harm we rightly have a negative response which has an emotional and perhaps behavioural aspect to it as well as a cognitive one: I know that was wrong and feel it and want to do something about it. Read carefully, however, Jesus' teaching encourages us to see that in context. If we are short-changed by someone hawking cheap goods on the street shortly after inheriting a significant legacy then we should see the bigger picture and forget about it. If, on the other hand, we are being abused by a bully, the situation is very different.

It might help us to understand this vital aspect of Jesus' teaching if we see it as having to do with *integrity*. When we understand and feel that God loves us, we are drawn by the gravitational pull of the divine love to become in some way worthy of that love. We cannot earn or deserve it, but we desire to respond to it, to reciprocate in a small way. The changes that follow from this are what we call 'repentance'. When we repent of our sins, God forgives us. When God forgives us, we are given a fuller vision of the transcending love of God and this informs the way we view and relate to others; we see ourselves as unworthy again and we repent further, and so it goes on. But this cycle is not merely one of spiritual self-regard, it is social and those who truly repent look, love and long outwards.

God's forgiving love draws us into a gracious, creative spiral of love and forgiveness. This spiral has transformative power and is a contrary dynamic to the downward spiral of vengeful violence in which each injustice is met with a matching or worse reprisal. Jesus' teaching on forgiveness is intended not to demand that we forgive when we cannot but to draw us away from the dynamic of evil and into the dynamic of love and to let *that* dynamic inform and influence who we are both in the depths of our being and in our actions and attitudes. None of this means that in every situation of unjust harm there is a simple Christian response called 'forgiveness'.

For instance, what attitude should a follower of Jesus adopt towards someone who is oppressing or abusing him or her in an ongoing way? It is vital to appreciate that that question cannot be resolved by a simple appeal to Jesus' words as if they meant that we must always forgive everyone instantly no matter what they do or how they feel about doing it. However, Jesus' teaching does not leave us free simply to adopt an ethic of reprisal or to respond with bitterness and hatred until the oppression stops and the former oppressor appears before us full of regret and begging for mercy. Rather, every follower of Jesus has the task of developing a forgiving heart. It is this forgiving heart, this disposition to forgive when possible, that is the attitude which Jesus seeks to inculcate in his followers and which Paul seeks to establish as the ethos of Christian gatherings or churches.

It is a challenge which is put before Christian people at their baptism and when they gather at the Lord's Table to celebrate the Eucharist. Indeed the development of such a forgiving heart lies at the core of Christian spirituality. It is not a second-order project – first get your beliefs straight and second learn how to be merciful while not giving up on the claims of justice. Becoming a forgiving person is the essence of Christian spiritual formation and as such involves knowing that we are not God and so opening ourselves to God and allowing God to work in and through us. The question becomes not 'can I forgive this or that harm?' but, 'what are the options under these circumstances (some degree of hurt inflicted by another) for me as a person with a forgiving heart, a person through whom God's spirit might work?'

Where, then, does that leave us in thinking about the Amish forgiveness after the Nickel Mines murders? The story from Nickel Mines is a powerful and positive one. The community did a noble thing by reaching out to the family of the gunman. They showed a very well developed forgiving spirit. But strictly speaking that was not *forgiveness*. Those people were not guilty of anything other than association with the murderer. We rightly admire the generosity of spirit seen here and recognize the spiritual and emotional maturity required to think about the needs of others when you and your community are in shock and grief. But to describe this as forgiveness is to stretch the language. Again that's not to criticize the spirit of what is happening. It is an admirable expression of a loving spirit and forgiving ethos. Impressive and moving as the story is, however, a different story would have been less than Christian.

Had the man's family been the subject of reprisals or revenge we would have doubted the moral reasoning involved and the spirituality of the community. Equally, had they been simply ignored that might have been harsh and cold. What made the story exceptional was not, I suggest, that something called 'forgiveness' happened but that the communal arrangements of the Amish established both clear boundaries and distinctive expectations of each other which, over the years, formed the social and personal habits of the heart which meant that in the aftermath of such a shocking and disorienting atrocity admirable and distinctive Christian behaviour emerged. There is no doubt that to visit and befriend that family was to engage in action that was at one with the ethics of the sermon on the mount and the spirit of the Beatitudes but also the qualities which Paul urges on the Colossians and Ephesians and which he describes as the 'fruit of the spirit' when writing to the Galatians.[9]

The situation which the Amish faced, while terrible, was neither impossible nor ambiguous. It feels cruel to suggest it, but they may have been tested even more deeply. Let us suppose that the situation had been different and that the man in question had not murdered and committed suicide, but had abducted one or more of the girls to a nearby farm. Suppose further that he had abused and tortured her before killing her and had then emerged without a hint of repentance? The situation is unspeakable, but not sadly, impossible. The question that it forces on us is what the imperative to forgive which we find in Jesus' teaching might mean in such a situation. It is the sort of question that begins to tear individuals and communities apart. In such a situation, forgiveness is going to be at least a struggle and probably a matter of anguish and agony.

To understand the New Testament properly we must not allow ourselves to think that there is a simple and admirable course of action for such a situation which is called 'forgiveness' and which the better Christian person will somehow achieve. It is both more realistic and more possible to pose the question 'what will a person with a forgiving heart experience in such a situation?' I am sure it is not possible to answer these questions in terms of words on a page that might apply in all, or even most, cases. All we can do is point inarticulately in the direction of the wilderness of hurt and say that they will have been taken to a particularly desolate part of that dread (but not dead) landscape. Honesty demands accepting it; faith and hope insist that this is not the end of the story.

A simplistic reading of the challenge to be forgiving in Matthew 18 and the Lord's Prayer can lead us into some very dangerous waters. Taken literally, they might suggest that the ideal response would be to reach out with forgiveness to an unrepentant torturing murderer during and after his actions. But this is absurd. As long as the harm is being committed the priority must be to stop it. When it is stopped the primary concerns are grief and justice. It is impossible to say how any community would respond to this but they would be acting wisely if they attended to the grief that flowed from this situation among themselves and assist the police in making arrests and pressing charges. My worry for any who take the imperative to forgive which they read in the New Testament out of context is that they are likely to distress themselves further because they realize that they do not have the capacity to forgive in the situation in which they find themselves.

The reality is that it *is* very difficult indeed for the forgiving heart to know what to feel or do in such situations. They are profoundly overwhelming and utterly shattering. But maybe that is the beginning of the answer. Maybe the forgiving heart makes its presence felt not by assuming a God-like power of pardon but by accepting the experience of overwhelming agony and confusion. The forgiving victim wants to be able to forgive the evil-doer and rehabilitate them to the path of goodness, but the suffering inflicted (or which is still being inflicted) is an outrage to the victim's dignity and an affront to justice. All that makes forgiveness seem out of the question, and yet for the forgiving heart, forgiveness is important, and at some level desirable, even when it is impossible. That's the agony.

It does not mean that come what may, however bad, hurtful or unfair, the Christian's first duty is to come up with this gift which puts it all right. This is a very important point and must be emphasized for two very significant reasons. One is that it simply can't be done and the other is that in trying to do it the would-be forgiver not only does themselves enormous harm, they also harm the guilty person and the social context and human community of which they are a part.

The Christian imperative to forgive is a spiritual one. It does not mean that 'whatever happens you must now forgive completely and fully'. Rather it means that the distinctive Christian virtues and the 'fruit of the spirit' are always relevant. Quite how they apply, and the extent to which they can bring personal healing and then some kind of forgiveness or reconciliation to a situation, will vary from place to place, time to time, context to context. We must always remember that Paul wrote for a specific situation and so when he writes to the Colossians that they must 'bear with one another' and 'if anyone has a complaint against another, forgive each other' (Colossians 3.13) he is not talking about what we have called the higher levels of harm or hurt.

The words, 'forgive each other; just as the Lord has forgiven you, so you also must forgive' (3.13) speak absolutely of the dynamics that are integral to the life of any church. They are about the ethos that should prevail and the generosity of spirit that should appertain between people who are of good will and pursuing a path of repentance and mutual forgiveness. They are simply not relevant to the situation where cruelty is visited on oneself or on a loved one. What we do not have is Paul's letter to the community of Nickel Mines, nor his advice to those whose children have been abducted or to a support group of victims of rape or childhood abuse or parents or siblings of murdered children. It is a spiritual and ethical mistake to suggest that we have.

But suppose we did! Presumably the message would retain a strong emphasis on forgiveness but it might take the form of, 'come what may, you must be forgiving; both forgiving people and a forgiving community'. It might go on to say, 'even in situations where it seems impossible to forgive, you must retain that forgiving heart'. If it did, the corollary would be plain, whether or not it would be written into the text of the letter itself: that a forgiving heart will often be challenged and sometimes it will be broken and torn apart. At such times forgiveness will be something that emerges slowly from a heart which is prepared to experience the tension between the simultaneous impossibility and necessity of forgiveness.

## Words, Parables and Stories

Interpreting the duty to forgive, not as a requirement to forgive instantly or completely, but rather as a spiritual duty to develop a forgiving heart and sustain a forgiving ethos in our communities, helps us be much more realistic about forgiveness between people. In order to sustain such a positive and creative perspective we do need, however, to remain clear about the difference between human forgiveness and divine forgiveness and that between God and human beings.

Unfortunately there are elements of what we might call the methodology of the Christian gospel which incline us to get these things muddled. A brief look at some of Jesus' teaching about forgiveness can help to clarify this vital point. First, however, we should consider the two Greek words which appear in the New Testament, both of which are translated 'forgiveness'. One of them is the word *aphesis* which means 'to let go from an obligation or guilt or punishment'. The core meaning of the word suggests that its main task is not to refer to ways of dealing with the aftermath of bad actions but with something more broadly connected with healing and liberation.

As Fraser Watts has put it, '*aphesis* is about liberation at the deepest level; it is not about moral shortcomings'.[10] *Aphesis* is a noun. The verb form, *aphiemi*, covers a range of meanings including the 'letting go' we have already mentioned. It can also mean 'cancel' or 'remit' and is often used to refer to the cancellation of debts. Despite the distinction we have repeatedly made, it can mean either 'pardon' or 'forgive'. All these words have a legitimate place somewhere in the forgiveness family of concepts.

The other word which is translated as 'forgiveness' is *charizomai*. It is only found in the writings of Paul but it is in some ways more like the modern words used for forgiveness in several European languages in that it hides within itself the word and idea of *gift*. We can easily find 'give' in the middle of 'for-give-ness'. The word 'pardon' ends in three letters which we find both in the English word 'donation' and the French word 'donner' meaning 'to give'. In the New Testament the word for 'gift' is a more theologically charged word than in our modern European languages. It is the word 'charis' which is usually translated not 'gift' but 'grace'. We fail to understand the power of the word forgiveness or forgive when we fail to notice the 'give' in the middle. As we saw earlier, Jill Scott coined the word 'forgifting' in order to draw attention to the extraordinary, enigmatic and largely unconscious gift that any act of forgiveness represents.[11]

Words in isolation, however, can only offer glimpses of meaning. That is why Jesus, like many great teachers, often taught by telling stories. In Luke's gospel we find that three of his greatest ones attract the attention of anyone interested in forgiveness: the prodigal son, Zaccaheus, and the woman who anoints Jesus at the house of Simon the Pharisee. As stories of interpersonal forgiveness, however, they have less to teach us than is often supposed.

Take the story of the prodigal son. The drama is of the wandering and repentance of the younger son, the reacceptance of the father and the contrasting response of the elder brother, so full of grudging negativity. In terms of forgiveness, the story is primarily about the way in which God forgives those who have behaved self-indulgently and irresponsibly and the difficulty which more upright human beings have in accepting this. We will later see both that there is truth about forgiving to be learnt from identifying with the father and that doing so has its own dangers and difficulties. For now we should note that the relationship of father and wayward son is not the only or ordinary relationship between those who might be challenged to forgive each other. The story tells us very little about sons forgiving fathers or forgiveness between peers or strangers. At the level of human beings it is less a story about human forgiving and more a story about human repentance.

A different but related story is that of Zacchaeus, the tax collector who climbed the tree to see Jesus as he was teaching, and whom Jesus had visited at home (Luke 19.1-10). Zacchaeus had not repented at this time but Jesus reached out to him with gracious acceptance – Jesus became his guest – and as a result, Zacchaeus was touched and transformed. His repentance, his change of attitude and behaviour, came in response to this visit. He gave away half his possessions to the poor and guaranteed to repay fourfold anyone he had defrauded. It is another story, as Jesus' comment at the end of the story makes clear, of the lost being found.[12] It is a pity, as it so often is, that the gospel writers' interest is so focused on Jesus that he does not tell us what happens to Zacchaeus later and we do not know whether those whom he repaid with so much interest either accepted it or forgave him. Nor do we know whether Zacchaeus himself became a forgiving person as a result of this encounter.

The story of Jesus being anointed at the house of Simon the Pharisee does enter more deeply into some of the human dynamics of forgiveness. But it is not a forgiveness story *per se*, rather a story of how the experience of forgiveness impacts on someone.[13] The woman expresses generous and extravagant love because this is what she has experienced. Simon the Pharisee is critical and Jesus tries to help him understand the ways of the heart by telling him a story about two debtors who have been let off respectively large and small debts. Jesus then makes Simon acknowledge that the one who is forgiven more will be proportionally more grateful.

The woman expresses deeper gratitude, understood as 'greater love', because she has been forgiven much. Those who have been forgiven little, by contrast, and the contrast here is with Simon, love meanly. Then there is another twist. Jesus affirms that her sins are forgiven but we cannot tell from the text whether this means that they are *now* forgiven, because Jesus says so, or that it is evident from her loving behaviour that she is a person who knows that she *has been* deeply forgiven.

I have come to the slightly ironic conclusion that this ambiguity is perhaps one of the more helpful ways in which forgiveness stories in the gospels can illuminate our understanding of interpersonal forgiveness. Often we cannot put hard and fast rules on what is first in the mutual processes of forgiveness, repentance and love. The deeper truth of the matter is that these three things are either all present or that none of them are present. Questions about order or priority, or even cause and effect, are essentially misplaced. That does not mean that it all happens in an intense instant. It does mean that the word 'process' is far too clunky and prosaic to describe what happens when we give and receive forgiveness.[14]

Another gospel story which is often referred to when the question of forgiveness arises is the one about the woman who is caught in the act of adultery. It appears in John 8 and although many scholars do not believe that it is an original part of John's gospel it is a very well known and much quoted story when it comes to forgiveness. The setting is the temple. The poor woman is dragged in and Jesus is asked a question designed to test his loyalty to the Law of Moses. His response is to doodle in the dust with his finger. This is certainly enigmatic. What is he up to? Giving himself some thinking time perhaps. Or maybe he is ignoring them and hoping they would drift off. But they keep badgering away and in the end he gets to his feet. 'He straightened up,' is what is written. We can imagine the unfolding of the full authority of the young rabbi. Then a pause, and then the witty response: 'Let anyone among you who is without sin be the first to throw a stone at her' (John 8.7). Then Jesus folds himself up again and gets back to the serious business of doodling in the dust. Shamefacedly they drift off, mindful of their own sin.

Once again we might helpfully ask whether this really is a forgiveness story. The only question which has been resolved is whether anyone thinks they are in a position to deliver the punishment. The woman is spared. Why? She has said nothing, confessed nothing and shown no contrition. She is spared not because anyone actively forgives her but because no one has the nerve to punish her. It tells us that Jesus was not inclined to prosecute the law. 'Has no one condemned you?' he asks. 'Neither do I… Go your way, and from now on do not sin again' (John 8.11). Given that John's gospel incorporates the longest conversation in the Bible, when Jesus talks with the Samaritan woman at the well in John 4, it is disappointing that he has not recorded more in this story.

Did Jesus go on to say, 'I don't want to know what you did but can you tell me why you did it? Did you not think of the man's family – and yours? Or am I assuming too much? Were you the victim here? Was this in reality more of a rape than an act of adultery?' If only he had opened up some of these issues with her and we had her answers. With that sort of information we might be able to say whether this really was a forgiveness story or not. As it is, what we have is story about Jesus outwitting the scribes and Pharisees and letting the woman go free with the warning: 'Sin no more.' This is only a forgiveness story if we think of 'not condemning' someone as a form of forgiving them.

Finally, we briefly turn to the story of the healing of the paralytic man who is lowered through a roof by his friends (Mark 2.1-12; Matthew 9.2-8; Luke 5.17-26). The language of forgiveness is definitely and deliberately used here but not in an interpersonal sense. Jesus does not forgive the man in the way that a victim might forgive someone who is responsible for their harm. This is not 'victim forgiveness'. Jesus rather is claiming the authority to forgive sins as 'son of man'. By doing so he is undermining the authority of the religious authorities and the system of temple sacrifices. This subversive intent is evident in several cases where there is a suggestion from others that a healing issue might be a forgiveness issue. For instance, there is the story in John's gospel of the healing of the man born blind. The disciples ask: 'Who sinned, this man or his parents?' Jesus replies that neither sinned and does not refer to forgiveness at all when he heals him (John 9).

In a similar vein, although blind Bartimaeus pleads for 'mercy' Jesus asks him what he (really) wants. There is no mention of forgiveness when Jesus restores his sight (Mark 9.52; Luke 18.35-43). In all these examples, Jesus is, as it were, 'freeing' forgiveness from its religious captivity and while that is relevant to the way in which we might come to think about the nature of God's forgiveness and the central importance not of ritual but of repentance, it does not directly add to our understanding of interpersonal forgiveness.

## Reflection

The question of how to handle and interpret the New Testament imperative to forgive is one of immense significance for victims of unjust harm or hurt. The more intense or destructive the harm, the higher the level of hurt, the more sensitive and difficult it is to get the message right. However, if the interpretation that I am offering here is convincing, it opens the door to an understanding of the imperative or duty to forgive which is not only realistic and demanding but also intelligible and, in a certain way, possible. For some it will involve a certain amount of 'un-thinking' or, put more positively, 're-imagining'.

The Christian duty to forgive is not one which involves victims of serious hurt imagining that they now have God-like powers of absolution which they, as victim, can choose to withhold or discharge. Rather it is the duty of Christian people to develop a forgiving heart, characterized by the distinctive virtues, and for Christian communities to nurture and sustain a forgiving ethos. That involves engaging with forgiveness neither as a primarily ethical issue, nor one of the exercise of authority, but as a matter of ongoing and everyday spirituality.

One of our most serious concerns in this book is the question of what happens to the person with a forgiving heart when they are put into a situation where forgiveness seems impossible. What we have so far considered of the New Testament does not prepare people for this. There is no suggestion that there are times when forgiveness is *off* the agenda. But forgiveness between people is not *on* the agenda as often as is sometimes supposed. The way in which Jesus talked about forgiveness, and offered it, are not as relevant to the subject as we may have been led to suppose. Any duty regarding forgiveness is best understood not as a requirement to forgive come what may, so much as the challenge to engage with whatever life throws at us with a forgiving heart and to allow ourselves to be drawn into the spiritual struggle and healing agony which is honest about hurt and hopeful about overcoming the emotional and spiritual damage inflicted by others.

## Notes

1. Kraybill, D. B., Nolt, S. M., Weaver-Zercher D. L. *Amish Grace: How Forgiveness Transcends Tragedy*, p. 95.
2. Williams, C. *He Came Down From Heaven and The Forgiveness of Sins*, p. 157.
3. Williams, C. *He Came Down From Heaven and The Forgiveness of Sins*, p. 165.
4. Stephen's words, 'Lord, do not hold this sin against them' (Acts 7.60)

contrast strongly with those of Zechariah son of Jehoiada who, as he was being stoned to death for speaking out prophetically, said, 'May the Lord see and avenge.' (2 Chronicles 24.22)

5. All Biblical quotations are from the New Revised Standard Version.
6. Anthony Bash makes this point by turning on its head the argument of philosopher Anne Minas who says that God cannot forgive in the way that humans forgive. Bash, A. *Just Forgiveness*, pp. 26–27.
7. Wright, N. T. *Evil and the Justice of God*, p. 103–4.
8. Bash, A. *Just Forgiveness*, p. 67.
9. 'Love, joy, peace, patience, kindness, generosity, faithfulness, gentleness and self-control' (Galatians 5.22).
10. Watts, F. *Forgiveness in Context*, p. 55.
11. See above, p. 23
12. 'The Son of Man came to seek out and to save the lost' (Luke 19.10).
13. The sins and offences are off the page and it is not clear whom they are against. There is no confession. The tears could be tears of contrition, but perhaps they are tears of gratitude. That's one of the things about feelings that are not expressed in words. You can never be sure of the meaning. But then again forgiveness does not always happen through a clearly articulated process or through a transaction where everyone is clear about what everyone else means or intends. Ambiguity is part of the territory of forgiveness.
14. Paul van Tongeren has suggested that the apparent impossibility of forgiveness might be explained as its intersubjectivity. He uses the example of a greeting to make his point. I cannot greet you unless I raise my hand in a gesture (or something similar) but I will not have greeted you unless you acknowledge and respond to my wave. Thus greeting cannot be unidirectional or happen in an instant – and yet to call greeting a *process* is to make it too mechanical. See van Tongeren, P. 'Impossible Forgiveness' in Bloch-Schulman, S. and White, D (eds) *Forgiveness: Probing the Boundaries*, p. 45.

## CHAPTER 5

# Anger, Resentment and Grudge

When conducting a parish retreat on the subject of forgiveness, I invited participants to list some of the different expressions that are commonly used to express the state of being angry. I only had to ask and they came tumbling out: 'my blood boiled', 'I was spitting feathers', 'I was furious', 'he saw red', and 'she flew off the handle'. I was surprised by just how many such expressions we came up with between us. But I was even more surprised how much the participants enjoyed themselves. They loved it; there was real energy in the room. Anger is not only an emotion but a cathartic emotion. It can have a cleansing and healing effect; it can get something 'out of our system'.

The New Testament, like the Old, is not, perhaps surprisingly, against anger. While the Bible warns against letting anger persist or develop into something worse, it accepts it as a fact of life. When Paul, writing to the Ephesians says, 'be angry but do not sin' he is quoting Psalm 4.4 and in both cases it is not anger itself that is bad, it's what it can all too easily lead to. I once invited a rabbi along to a Bible study group. We were soon talking about Jesus: 'What a temper that man had,' was his comment. We are often tempted to airbrush Jesus' anger (or Paul's) out of the New Testament. But we cannot do so without distorting their passion or personality. Anger, it seems, is integral to seeking God's kingdom.

Anger is a complex emotion, laden with the potential to be destructive but also to be a force for good. The danger is that when we are angry we feel both strong and righteous and so we drop our defences and become vulnerable. Anger threatens to boil over into aggression before we fully appreciate what is going on. Anger is self-forgetful in a bad way. When we are angry our attention focuses on the present moment and we desire to deal with the cause of our irritation or harm so intensely that we forget the possibility of consequences – whether for the person whom we are about to lash out at, whether verbally or physically, or for ourselves. Our wider judgement is impaired and we take risks that we would not countenance if we were not so furious. We say things we would not say on a calmer occasion and we run the risk of upsetting people with our uncharacteristically blunt and disrespectful words.

On the other hand, anger can connect with courage. It can make us brave and it is not unknown for those training soldiers or participants in contact sports to provoke them to anger. It is a risky strategy because anger and wisdom, it seems, are in inverse proportion. If anger gets to a certain pitch then courage becomes foolhardiness and passion for victory tips into reckless disregard for the rules of engagement. It is angry sports players who find themselves sent to the sin-bin. But that does not mean that all anger is sinful. The idea of appropriate or proportional anger does make sense.

Anger is a pre-reflective reaction to a situation. A surge of adrenalin has been precipitated for some reason (our blood has boiled) and we choose not to run or fly but to stand and fight. This makes anger an unreliable emotion. It can be triggered by many things. Just because we are angry it does not mean that someone has done wrong, or that an injustice has been perpetrated. The reality might be that we are mistaken as to what has happened, or why, or that we are an ill-tempered, irascible person who is always 'flying off the handle'. In such a case, talk of forgiveness is quite inappropriate.

Martha Nussbaum has convincingly argued that emotions can be intelligent and that we should therefore pay them attention, *read* them, as it were, and respond to the intuitions and perceptions that they carry and hold.[1] Nonetheless, anger can undermine our capacity to pay attention to all the relevant information and to weigh it carefully before acting. Anger management is a common psychological treatment for people who are in the habit of having a disproportionately angry response to situations or who act out their anger violently. But there is more to forgiving than managing our anger. Because when we forgive we have to overcome the anger which is appropriate, the anger which is an 'intelligent' response to injustice.

In the play *The Long Road*, Mary is the mother of an eighteen-year-old boy who has been murdered in a random stabbing incident. In a short soliloquy she expresses the rage she feels and how she imagines acting it out:

> D'ya know I've imagined beating her [Emma, the murderer] to death with a baseball bat. I've imagined setting her on fire, shooting her, running her over in a tank. Things that scare me, things I've never felt before, never imagined before. There's this kaleidoscopic rage inside me, and I realise I could kill someone. She kills my son, so I kill her, I wipe her off the face of the earth. I could do it. Truly.[2]

For Mary, the anger takes expression as fantasized revenge. Revenge is almost the oldest story in the book; it is the story of Cain and Abel (Genesis 4.1-16). But it can be illustrated by many more recent examples. The plot of the 1992 film *Unforgiven* is driven by the desire for revenge, vengeance and retribution. The tragedy is that although the leading character, William Munny, seems to have been weaned away from violence by the love of his wife, after her early death from smallpox, poverty and opportunity conspire to draw him back into a tragic cycle of violence.

He, together with his old friend, Ned, have a history of killing, but by the time we meet them in the film, neither of them has the appetite for violence that they once had. Ned in fact turns home from the killing mission at the centre of the film because he realizes that he can no longer pull the trigger of his rifle when there is a man in the sights. On his way back he is captured and dies in the course of a brutal interrogation. When William hears of this he takes a drink of whiskey and the old violent, vengeful self returns to dominate his actions.

Commenting on this film in *Embodying Forgiveness*, Gregory Jones suggests that its darkest aspect is the suggestion that 'we are so thoroughly habituated to violence that we now are incapable of unlearning it'.[3] I do not see it in quite that way. For me, the film speaks of the struggle between vengeful and merciful responses to situations that outrage. In the incident which sparks the story off, a prostitute is savagely attacked by a client who, though he does not kill her, inflicts disfiguring wounds. To the irritation of the woman's colleagues and friends, the local sheriff declines to whip him. Rather he fines him so that the owner of the bar where she works might receive some compensation for his financial loss – her capacity to earn for him having been much reduced by her disfigurement. When the man returns with the required fine of ponies he also brings an extra pony, the best, as a gift for the woman herself. But it is scorned and he is sent from the town in a hail of stones and abuse. Revenge, anger and retribution vie with mercy and compassion both in the story and in the minds and the hearts of the protagonists.

This tension between justice and mercy, retribution and compassion, is never easy, and neither the way in which things work out, nor the emotions which actually lead to the decisive action, can be prejudged. Both event and character have unpredictable influences. It is in this way, I suggest, that the film has much to teach us about vengeance and forgiveness. The difference between them is enormous in quality and consequences, but which road is taken is the product of a complex mix of reactions, dispositions, events, company, character, personal history and hopes. It is this complex that we need to navigate wisely if we are to ever make sense of forgiveness in our lives.

The causes of anger can be very diverse and people can vary enormously in the way they respond to different triggers. To take a very different example, Jean Twenge and Keith Campbell argue in their book *The Narcissism Epidemic* that in today's world, unreasonable levels of what they call 'entitlement' and desire for fame can make a significant contribution to the tendency to behave aggressively towards others. They focus on people with very high levels of self-regard, whom they call narcissists:

> Narcissists are aggressive exactly because they love themselves so much and believe that their needs take precedence. They lack empathy for other people's pain and often lash out when they feel they aren't getting the respect they deserve – and they often deserve a lot because they are, of course, better than everyone else.[4]

The internal logic of this is compelling. For the narcissist, others are competitors for respect, status, consumer goods and the most prized of 'goods' – fame. This is a dangerous situation because in terms of sheer probability narcissists are very likely to be frustrated in their desire and yet they do not have a narrative or context to explain why. They will also lack good friends who can be honest with them, because as narcissistic people they place little value on close emotional relationships. Indeed the condition of narcissism could be described as the absence of a personal understanding of one's place with and alongside others; that is, a personal theory of humility.

Frustrated narcissists are likely to be angry people but they are not going to be helped by forgiveness because their frustration is not a product of injustice. It is their egotistical expectations and naïve hopes rather than their experiences which are unjust. Angry with the world as it is, they miss the point. It is the world as it is that is *real*. It's not the world that needs to change but the narcissist; or rather, it is the narcissistic trait in each one of us that needs to be challenged.

The proper focus of irritation is sometimes our own misguided desires. To encourage an angry narcissist to forgive the world for not meeting their naïve and vain hopes of celebrity is neither sensible nor kind; it is, in fact, simultaneously to enrage and encourage them. The message to the narcissist, and indeed to the narcissistic side of each person, is not 'forgive' but 'repent'. It is not every form of anger which is helped by forgiving. It only makes sense to forgive when someone is at fault. But as we have seen, forgiveness is not just a method to help the angry to have a more peaceful life, anger itself is important.

Anger is a difficult and dangerous emotion. It shouts at us and we cannot always be sure that we want to hear what it is saying. But I have drawn attention to narcissistic anger and the anger that boils over into vengeance and violence not in order to suggest that anger is always bad, but to clarify that it is sometimes bad. The implication of this is also important. Sometimes anger is the right feeling to have. Anger can be honest and passionate and appropriate. It can flare up in the face of injustice, abuse and disrespect. It can light a fire in our hearts when we see others being maltreated or when we realize that we ourselves are not being dealt with justly.

Sometimes our anger will be a sign to us that our intuitions have realized that things are wrong, very wrong. Other times it will just be our ego having a fit of pique. Forgiveness calls us to be careful with our anger, and to discern its cause patiently and wisely. It also invites us to do something very strange and counter intuitive. It invites us, when we have ascertained for certain that our anger is justified, to give it up and move beyond it. Forgiveness does not invite us not to be angry. Rather it *requires* us to take the risk of anger when we recognize injustice.

## Resentment

So far I have been talking about anger as a hot emotion. But there are other forms and other words which describe similar but slightly different feelings. The most important of them is 'resentment'.

It is characteristic of healthy, hot or 'everyday' anger that it wears off after a while. But sometimes it does not. Sometimes it stays. It becomes settled. This settled anger is what we mean by words like 'resentment'. If we wind the clock back a few centuries and meet the eighteenth-century thinker Joseph Butler, we discover that he was much exercised by the subjects of resentment and forgiveness. In 1726, he published fifteen of the sermons he had preached at the Rolls Chapel in Chancery Lane, London. The sermon titles touch on many concerns which are important to us today: 'human nature', 'compassion', 'self-deceit', 'love of neighbour' and 'love of God', as well as those whose titles might surprise us or sound obscure such as, 'upon the government of the tongue' and 'upon the character of Balaam'. But at the heart of the collection lie two sermons which are still regularly quoted and argued about in ethical and theological writing: 'Upon Resentment' and 'Upon the Forgiveness of Injuries'.

In his sermon on resentment, Butler asks himself whether there is, in fact, some good to be found in resentment. He was motivated to do so because he believed that God must have planted the tendency to respond to injustice and hurt with resentment in our hearts for good reason. Butler concludes that resentment is the emotion of self-protection and that it is an appropriate emotional response when we observe or experience injustice. Such 'resentment against vice and wickedness', he argues, 'is one of the common bonds by which society is held together; a fellow feeling, which each individual has on behalf of the whole species, as well as of himself'.[5] For Butler resentment is, perhaps surprisingly, a good thing.

It is immensely helpful that Butler points to the positive side of resentment. One of the sad features of some so-called Christian teaching about forgiveness is that it fails to understand or accept this point. Forgiveness is portrayed as a response to wrongdoing, injury or offence which says, in effect, that 'what happened does not matter'. Butler's analysis prevents us making this simple but very common mistake; a mistake which replaces the virtuous practice of forgiveness with an easy tolerance and thereby turns people worthy of dignity and respect into the doormats of the powerful and wicked.

Resentment is a good thing because it is the emotional way in which we assert the importance of justice. It is with healthy resentment that we cry out against the wrong that has been inflicted on us or on one about whom we care. Whereas anger shouts out, 'No! This is not right. Arggg!', resentment is a more soulful and resolved feeling: 'This really is not right and should not have happened. I am not putting up with it.' Like anger, resentment can be a mouthpiece of justice but it speaks with a different tone of voice. Forgiveness does not require that we silence or ignore either but that we learn how to live with, and listen to, both while doing what we can to ensure that they do not get the last word.

Both hot anger and settled resentment have their dangers. But while the problem with anger is that we lose all sense of ourselves, and focus negatively on the other who has harmed us, the danger with resentment can be its self-absorption. We have already noted that there is a pleasure in anger, a pleasure which comes from an association with catharsis. Pleasure can also attach itself to resentment but far from this being a cathartic clear-out of our psychic space, it can become a form of mental clutter and emotional mess. Victims of serious unjust harm, especially if it is ongoing, are very vulnerable to such cluttering of their inner lives.

If, over time, resentment settles into the soul, life can be diminished both for the person holding them and for any with whom they might relate. This is where the idea of forgiveness as the 'forswearing of resentment' becomes so relevant.[6] It is also why those who advocate therapeutic forgiveness can produce evidence that forgiving is good for your physical and mental health.[7] Not all philosophers, however, are convinced that resentment is something that should be forsworn, given away or dismissed from our minds and hearts.

Jeffrie Murphy is one of the clearest advocates today for the importance of holding on to resentment. In an essay arguing that the current vogue for forgiveness therapy needs to be moderated, he suggests that sometimes a failure to resent poor treatment can reflect an 'improperly low view of his or her moral status and dignity in the first place'.[8] As he puts it:

> Victims may be harmed symbolically as well as physically by those who wrong them. Wrongdoing is in part a communicative act, an act that gives out a degrading or insulting message to the victim – the message 'I count and you do not, and I may thus use you as a mere thing'. Resentment of the wrongdoer is one way that a victim may evince, emotionally, that he does not endorse this degrading message; in this way resentment may be tied to the virtue of self-respect.[9]

The consequence for Murphy is that a self-respecting person will not easily forgive. Rather they will want to see evidence of change in the offender. This view is challenged by some psychologists who argue that to act on this basis means that victims must suffer twice. Their view is that, since there is nothing that can now be done about the hurtful event in the past, the wise victim will want to free themselves from the troubling emotions like resentment and from any fantasies of revenge. For them 'forgiveness' is liberation from the unpleasant psychological consequences of hurtful events in the past. They are concerned for people who are not only the victim of the original offence but also of the unpleasant experience of their own resentment of it. For them, 'to forgive is to show self-respect'.[10] Murphy tries to look sympathetically at this, but in the end rejects the possibility:

> In my view slavery, oppression and victimization are made worse, not better, when people are rendered content in their victimization. The counsel immediately to love, forgive, and turn the other cheek may be justified in certain versions of

Christian theology, but I am not at all sure that it is always good advice for counsellors to give to victims.[11]

Quoting Marx's famous view about religion as the opiate of the people, he shares his fear that forgiveness might sometimes work like a drug that helps pacify people so that, rather than resenting their treatment, they collude with their oppressors, aggressors and violators.

We could go deeper into this argument but it may not be necessary. Clearly there are victims and victims. That is why I have suggested that we think in terms of different levels of hurt. However, Murphy is calling to mind something other than the degree of hurt. He is interested in whether or not the abuse or harm is ongoing. His point is that if someone is in a situation where they are being repeatedly harmed and hurt or constantly oppressed then the forswearing of resentment is a bad idea. It is, we might add, a failure to listen to what our uncomfortable and unpleasant feeling is saying to us.

His point is valid. It would be strange to counsel someone who is in an ongoing and dangerously abusive relationship to forgive the person hurting them and to assist them in doing so could exacerbate the harm done. The right thing to do in such a situation, I would suggest, would be to help the person attend to their own resentment and discern whether it is in fact the voice of justice, and, if so, let it guide and inform their actions carefully. There are two dangers in such a situation. One is that by failing to resent the abuser, the victim not only continues to suffer themselves but also makes it more likely that others will suffer from the same person or people. The other is that they will one day come to the end of their capacity to tolerate and find that a relatively minor incident is 'the last straw' which leads to an angry and violent response. Many a domestic murder has come after years of suffering in silence.

There are real dangers when 'tolerance' extends to hurts that are more than trivial. It is possible to be too tolerant; to become so accustomed to ignoring things that irritate and annoy us that we fail to develop appropriate resentment when injustice is perpetrated. If we are too tolerant, too lazily nice, we end up inhibiting the emotions which tell us 'No! That was not just a nuisance, it was *wrong*!' On the other hand, not to try to help someone to let go of their still simmering indignation years after they were badly treated by a colleague at work, is also a mistake. Sometimes we should listen to, and act on, our resentment. Sometimes we should let it go. We need to be prudent and wise in order to be good forgivers but also in order to be good helpers to those who have in some way been unjustly hurt.

Although we think of resentment as a more settled emotion than anger, it is not as stable as we might sometimes imagine. It too changes over time and when resentment takes a more solid and enduring form we call it a 'grudge'. Grudges are unattractive but there is, I want to suggest, something to be said for them. That is, there can be good or appropriate grudges as well as bad ones. Indeed a good grudge is what is called for in the situation that Murphy describes: that is, one of settled injustice and ongoing harm, or oppression.

In the next section I argue that the oppressed are well advised to hold onto a grudge and that to do so is not necessarily to be unforgiving. On the other hand grudges, like anger and resentment, can be very dangerous. We can grow comfortable with them and even depend on their company to give us a sense of equilibrium. The specific danger of the grudge is that it poisons the personality and remains as a character trait after the conditions which made it appropriate have changed. A grudge might be a survival mechanism, but like a life jacket, when we are out of danger we are well advised to remove it.

## Grudges

A grudge is a specific form of resentment. They arise when we are unfairly hurt or diminished in some way over a period of time so that resentment has become an enduring aspect of our character. However, the word 'grudge', especially when in the form 'grudging', can also imply something more. For there is not only settled hurt or hidden anger in it but also something apparently *mean* about it. The word 'grudging' speaks of the opposite of generosity of spirit, or magnanimity. The offence of the elder brother in the story of the prodigal son (Luke 15) was not that he was a hard worker, nor was it that he was shocked by his father's generosity. His problem was that he could not come to terms with that generosity, or share in it. There was something irreducibly hard, 'un-melt-able', and mean-spirited about him. He was miserly with his good will. He held a grudge, and he held it tightly.

But grudges are not only about meanness. In order to understand grudges fully it is necessary, I suggest, to reflect on questions of power. One of the reasons that people offend or hurt each other is that people are seeking to establish, reinforce or exploit an inequality of power. Indeed much violence is about exactly this, and there are all sorts of non-physical – and yet hurtful – ways in which people put each other down. In these cases, the question is not so much, 'is forgiveness natural or simple?' but, 'is it wise?' The worry for those who forgive, and the reason for people turning their back on the way of forgiveness, is that it might give more power to those who oppress or exploit. Sometimes, therefore, it might be appropriate to develop a grudge. Consider these situations:

- A stranger throws a stone at your window and smashes it.
- Someone working in your home steals a small item.
- A friend repeatedly fails to meet up as arranged.
- Your spouse hits you while drunk.

In such situations the question is not so much what our initial response might be, but: what may the consequences be if we forgive it too easily or quickly. The most obvious danger is that the perpetrator will do it again, and that we, or someone else, will end up getting even more badly hurt. Because they 'get away with it' the perpetrator might slide more deeply into bad habits and end up in very serious trouble. If no one stands up to a bully they tend to continue in their bullying. This is the law of the playground, the workplace and the home. In these situations, the desire to forgive runs up against the desire to act responsibly and wisely and to keep yourself and others safe. Once again, the forgiving heart is agonized.

If we seek to forgive, we need to reflect about what we are forgiving and to ask whether we are making the world a better place or a worse place. Forgiveness is a psychological and spiritual process which has ineluctable ethical dimensions. In the situations described, it seems unlikely that it would be helpful to develop a grudge after just one incidence of harm, however much it irritates or annoys us. We could be angry about it; we might also resent it. However, if the offences were to be repeated, and the offending person was using this behaviour in order to dominate or oppress, then a grudge could be an appropriate response. Not the last word, perhaps, but part of the process of living with repeated unjust injury or settled oppression or exploitation.

Grudges are perhaps the least attractive responses to injustice but they may sometimes be justified and therefore preferable to forgiving too easily. Sometimes grudges exist not because people are mean-spirited but because they are trapped in oppressive and exploitative situations where there is no possibility of expressing or acting on their anger or resentment. Consider the case of slavery. One can hardly deny that a slave is in a position of being unjustly harmed. She might be being treated well (for a slave) but the harm and hurt is to her dignity, freedom and integrity as well as in being deprived of the fruits of her work.

We should, I suggest, think very carefully before suggesting that a slave who holds a grudge has an unforgiving heart or is in some way failing in forgiveness. Certainly we might think it ethically questionable if she plots to murder or maim those who are treating her well in a context where her hopes as a free individual would be limited. We might also be concerned for her spiritual or emotional well-being if she became consumed by hatred for her captors. But to begrudge her a grudge seems to be mean-spirited on the part of the observer. Hers is a well-advised grudge, a good grudge. A grudge that is not out of place in a forgiving heart.

But how do we know whether a grudge is a good one or a toxic one? It is, I suggest, a matter of context. As long as an oppressive situation persists then a grudge can be a good thing. However, if the situation changes then the forgiving person who has held a grudge will find a way to let go of it. A grudge is good only as long as an unjust situation continues. As soon as we hold a grudge because of what we *remember* then we are in a different territory. A good grudge becomes a bad grudge when it is a habit of heart or disposition of mind which has become firmly cemented into the character.

Sadly people can derive pleasure and comfort from their grudges, and they become content as grudge-bearers, making, perhaps, some core aspect of their identity out of it. They become friends with their grudge and feel that the grudge offers a reason or excuse for their uncharitable attitudes. The danger of nursing a grudge is parallel to the danger of failing to curb an explosive temper. We settle for the easy pleasure rather than engaging in the healing agony of forgiveness. But while temper is controlled by maturity or emotional self-control, grudges are given up when we forgive.

## Reflection

Anger and resentment are part of our emotional makeup for good reason. They are there to help us protect ourselves both physically and psychologically, that is, in terms of self-respect. But these justice-seeking emotions can in turn endanger us if we either fail to pay them careful attention or if we grow used to them as part of our makeup and daily experience. The difference is that while anger is a danger to us because of what might happen in the moment when it flares up, resentment is a danger to us if it becomes a bad grudge. But there are also good grudges which we develop when we are powerless to do anything about the injustice we experience or see inflicted on others.

This analysis of anger, resentment and grudges suggests a spectrum of injustice which ranges from a random incident (for example, being mugged while visiting a city where you are a stranger) to being the victim of systematic oppression (for example, being kept in slavery or exploited for very low wages). At the left is the zone of anger and to the right the zone of the grudge. Pure or complete forgiveness is more likely to be possible to the left of the spectrum. We are unjustly hurt. We experience the anger. We control it. Then we let it go because it has done its job of alerting our offender to the hurtful consequences of their actions. We can see their regret and remorse and trust that they do indeed respect us and intend not to repeat the offence. But the forgiving spirit can also operate, though with more subtlety and less satisfaction, at the other end of the spectrum. This time the offence is intentional and ongoing but rather than developing bitterness and hatred which plot revenge, the forgiving heart develops a good grudge and holds it only as long as necessary.

What these reflections make clear is that while forgiveness might involve letting go of anger and resentment in response to the regret and remorse of the offender, the person with a forgiving attitude or spirit has available other options than vengeance, hatred or bitterness. It is not always clear what those options are, but the analysis here suggests that angry episodes, and more extended periods of grudge-bearing, are not inconsistent with forgiveness in the wider sense. However, life is so complicated, and issues so multithreaded, that it seems fair to suggest that whenever we forgive we are doing something *creative* with unjust hurt, righteous anger, appropriate resentment. It even suggests that forgiving people will not be entirely grudge-free but that they will hold their grudges provisionally and lightly, letting them go when they have done their work.

## Notes

1. Nussbaum, M. C. *Upheavals of Thought*.
2. Stevenson, S. *The Long Road*, p. 16.

3. Jones, G. L. *Embodying Forgiveness*, p. 77.
4. Twenge, J. M and Campbell, W. K. *The Narcissism Epidemic*, p. 196.
5. Butler, J. *Butler's Fifteen Sermons Preached at the Rolls* Chapel, pp. 72–79.
6. Many writers attribute this definition to Bishop Butler. However, as Charles Griswold has pointed out Butler's understanding was that forgiveness is the forswearing of revenge. Griswold, C. L. *Forgiveness*, p. 20.
7. The health benefits of forgiving has been the subject of scientific research. The sorts of benefits that are found include: reduced stress, lower blood pressure, fewer symptoms of depression and anxiety, better relationships and a more positive sense of well-being.
8. Lamb, S. and Murphy, J. G. (eds) *Before Forgiving*, p. 45.
9. Lamb, S. and Murphy, J. G. (eds) *Before Forgiving*, p. 44.
10. Lamb, S. and Murphy, J. G. (eds) *Before Forgiving*, p. 45.
11. Lamb, S. and Murphy, J. G. (eds) *Before Forgiving*, p. 46.

## CHAPTER 6

# After Murder

In 2005 Anthony Walker was murdered in Liverpool. This is what his mother, Gee, said immediately after the conviction of her son's attackers:

> Unforgiveness makes you a victim and why should I be a victim? Anthony spent his life forgiving. His life stood for peace, love and forgiveness and I brought them up that way. I have to practise what I preach. I don't feel any bitterness towards them really, truly, all I feel is… I feel sad for the family.[1]

Consciously or not she was echoing the more famous words of Gordon Wilson of Enniskillen, Northern Ireland, whose daughter Marie was killed in the Remembrance Day bomb in 1987. He was with her when the bomb went off. Many heard the interview he gave to the BBC immediately afterwards:

> I said: 'Are you all right, dear?'… but we were under six feet of rubble… three or four times I asked her… she always said, 'Yes, I'm all right.'… I asked her the fifth time… 'Are you all right, Marie?'… She said, 'Daddy, I love you very much…' Those were the last words she spoke to me… I kept shouting, 'Marie are you all right?'… There was no reply… I have lost

> my daughter, but I bear no ill will, I bear no grudge… Dirty sort of talk is not going to bring her back to life.[2]

The journalist Alf McCreary who was later to write a book with Wilson about all this, described hearing him speak on the radio. 'As he began talking I became absolutely frozen, with a cup of tea halfway to my lips. I could not move. His words, and his tone of barely controlled anguish, were burning deep into my very being'.[3] Many others were also moved by what they heard. They were noticed partly because they were in such contrast to much of the rhetoric that was coming from Northern Ireland at the time.

Wilson's response was also given prominence in the Queen's Christmas broadcast six weeks later. His words have been much discussed, praised and critiqued, even providing the starting point for a secular philosophical account of forgiveness.[4] In my experience they are almost invariably mentioned in a question from the audience if there is talk about forgiveness. Sometimes the assumption behind the question is that Wilson found it relatively straightforward to forgive and so why make it all sound so complicated? More often, the question is based on the assumption that he forgave so quickly that he did not really know what he was saying – that he was in shock.

Both questions need answers. The answer to the first one is that forgiveness might, in a specific incident, be simple and straightforward for one particular person, but that does not mean that forgiveness itself is simple, straightforward or easy. Quite what makes it possible for one person to find that they can forgive is a combination of factors including their own character. But character is not the only factor; we do not know how Wilson would have responded in other circumstances.

He himself has written of the greater difficulty faced by those who live on with broken bodies in chronic pain, together with their families and any others who care for them. Nor do we know how he would have responded if his daughter had been captured and tortured before being put to death. I make these points not to cast doubt on Wilson's capacity to forgive but to highlight how little we know about any particular case where we are not personally involved and how dangerous it is to generalize from one half-understood situation.

Regarding the question as to whether he spoke before what had happened had really sunk in, my opinion is that Wilson did indeed know what he was saying but that he did not, as none of us could, fully appreciate how much of struggle it would be to live up to those words in the years that followed. For one thing, he could have had no idea of the extent to which his words would have struck a chord with people and caught their imagination. However, that enormous public response is a clue to what was really happening here.

Northern Ireland in the 1980s was a place of violence and counter violence, attack and reprisal. Each act of vengeance was met with an act of revenge in a seemingly endless and unstoppable spiral. Wilson knew that his words would be heard by the Protestant paramilitaries. People in those organizations rarely heard words of forgiveness or mercy. All the pressure was to stoke up hatred and to incite people to further violence. By speaking as he did in the interview, Wilson was saying, to quote a slogan that came to prominence in another context, '*not in my name* will any vengeance be sought'.

He said that he held no ill will and, both as the father of one of the victims who had been killed, and as a person who was also personally harmed, his words, and, as McCreary's account of hearing the interview suggests, his *voice*, carried a certain authority. It was the radio broadcast of the interview that really connected with people, that really spoke. That man was there and *this* is how he responds. What people heard from Wilson was hope and dignity just as much as anguish and forgiveness. There was integrity too, because, over the years, Wilson remained true to his word:

> When I think directly of the people responsible for killing Marie and others, I don't bear them nasty thoughts. I am certainly not lying in my bed at night worrying about them. As human beings they have their own bits and pieces to pick up, and it's not for me to think ill of them or to bear them a grudge.[5]

Wilson's words in the immediate aftermath of the bombing were contextual and political. They were not only a report on his inner state but a message to those all too willing to take reprisals. It is of interest to me that when discussing this story in England, I have found it difficult to persuade people of this point. They have not wanted to see Wilson's words in this context but have preferred to hear them simply as a direct and intimate report on his attitude towards the murderers. This is true both for those who have admired his words ('it's truly wonderful') and of those who have been critical ('he was speaking too soon'). Commentators from Ireland, on the other hand, appreciate and make the same point. David Bolton writes that, 'his intervention at a time of considerable danger in the history of the civil conflict in Northern Ireland was widely regarded as instrumental in minimizing reprisal attacks'.[6]

But the words also generated controversy close to home. Aileen Clinton, whose mother Alberta also died in the bomb later said '[Gordon Wilson] never said he forgave. Has everybody else started saying that? To me it is morally indefensible to forgive people who aren't sorry.'[7] Clinton's words draw attention to two questions. First, is forgiveness possible in the absence of 'repentance' and second, might forgiveness be said to have taken place in the absence of an explicit use of the word 'forgiveness'. The question of the role of repentance in forgiveness between people is of great significance. In this context, it is particularly important because the idea that forgiveness can only follow repentance is integral to the way in which most Protestants think about it in Northern Ireland:

> In the Northern Ireland Protestant mindset justice (and therefore forgiveness) is seen more in legalistic and punitive terms than, perhaps, in the Catholic scheme of things. Thereby many Protestants have real difficulty in offering anything that might be construed as letting the criminal off scot-free.[8]

This comment comes from an essay in a collection which explores the meaning and dynamics of forgiveness in Northern Ireland. Several other contributors to the same volume endorse the view that a close identification of forgiveness with a response to repentance has been problematic in Northern Ireland. David Bolton speaks of the 'theological protocols of forgiveness' which have 'encumbered' public discourse.[9] David Clements writes that the question of forgiveness is 'vexed' because a transactional view of it requires apology, repentance and if possible restitution but 'in Northern Ireland there is little chance that many victims will ever receive an apology'.[10]

Such a view of forgiveness means that victims are effectively robbed of a possible means of empowerment and peace making. If forgiveness is impossible in the absence of repentance it raises the question of what moral and wise options remain for them.

This in turn depends on what the prevailing 'mind-set' believes is the appropriate response to the inflicting of pain, suffering and death. This leads on to the second question. It is true that Wilson did not say 'I forgive them' but he did say, 'I bear no ill will, I carry no grudge'.

I continue to admire Wilson for his choice of words and tone of voice that day. By avoiding the word 'forgive' but by declaring that he had no ill will he was beginning to open up a new and fertile space for moral creativity which might break the cycle of violence and open out to a new kind of future. Had he used the word 'forgiveness' or said, 'I forgive the bombers' he would have taken a step too far. Does this mean that people were wrong to interpret his words as forgiving? Again one has to be careful as the atmosphere around the word and the context is so charged. What I think he did was to give evidence of a forgiving spirit or a forgiving heart.

In 1990 Wilson wrote that he had no desire to meet the bombers. His wife Joan, on the other hand, wanted to speak to them and to demand an answer: 'Why? What is your justification for such acts?' In writing about forgiveness, Wilson is consistent and constant regarding his own position: 'I was not angry at the time and am not angry now.'[11] This too raises questions. We have explored the importance of moral anger, an emotional response to a situation that rages at injustice and the suffering that has been caused. The case for thinking this way is very strong and it inevitably leads to an ethical discussion about the grounds on which such moral anger might be overcome in an act of forgiveness.

Wilson's comment on not feeling anger has caused people to wonder about the moral integrity of his remarks. Once again this needs to be seen in context. Human beings are all different and emotional responses vary from person to person. It is conceivable that someone has moral repugnance without the often associated feelings of anger or rage. The question is not what they *feel* but what they *do*. Someone who inhabited an ethical framework which prized revenge would not be expected to denigrate a person who lived out the motto, 'don't get mad, get even'. Similarly with forgiveness, it might be unusual but it is not impossible to imagine someone reacting to such an event not with anger but with resigned sadness. This too is connected with contextual issues.

Wilson had lived through the Troubles for many years and had, we might assume, experienced many emotions as he heard of atrocity after atrocity. At one level the Enniskillen bomb added no new facts, no new data to the situation. Strong emotions come when human beings experience disorienting change, when the plot of life, as it were, changes in a way we have not anticipated. It is sad to say, but the story of the Troubles did not change when the Enniskillen bomb was detonated. It is just that the reality of it came home to the people of Enniskillen in the most intimate and horrible way possible.

Wilson was in the blast and held the hand of his dying daughter until she slipped away. Whether we attribute his lack of anger to exhaustion and weariness with it all or to a maturity which saw everything in the contextual way that I am suggesting does not really matter. What matters is that he channelled his energy first, into comforting his daughter and second, into finding words that were so surprising, sincere, generous, fresh and simple that they drew out a hopeful response from others. Crucially, they did not condone, tolerate or excuse. As his remarks about eternal judgement and what awaits the bombers reveal, he was not acquiescing in the face of evil, rather he was letting the sound of his forgiving heart, beating under enormous stress, be heard:

> Eleven people died in the tragedy. They cannot be brought back and they are all human beings, made like all of us in the image of God. Those who have to account for this deed will have to face a judgement of God which is way beyond the forgiveness of Gordon Wilson… Human beings may be, can be, and indeed ought to be, able to forgive on human terms, but ultimately it is for God to forgive, and on his terms.[12]

As he makes clear he was trying to behave as a forgiving person ('I hope that I am a man of a forgiving nature'[13]) and to live in a way which was consistent with the Lord's Prayer:

> We ask God to forgive us but we are always subjected to his condition that we must forgive those others... My words were not intended as a statement of theology or righteousness, rather they were from the heart, and they expressed exactly how I felt at the time, and as I still do.[14]

Wilson's impact in 1987 was enormous but the legacy of his words has been two-edged. His words were remarkable, surprising and *creative*. It was not a stock answer but the carefully crafted expression of creative integrity. As McCreary noted, it was not just the words, but the anguished voice. It all held together. When you heard the interview you encountered the heart of the man. Sadly the originality of what he said was gradually lost as it was reported over and over again until he was widely understood to have forgiven the bombers and to have set a moral example for victims of tragedy to follow.

There is irony in this if, as I have suggested, Wilsons' forgiving spirit was expressed in the creativity of what he said. It was not a formulaic response. It was not 'I forgive them.' It was more subtle, nuanced, surprising and important than that. Sadly this vivid and transforming moment has fuelled a trend of journalists to ask over-simplified questions of vulnerable people. These can include the invitation to articulate feelings which are still terribly raw but also questions about forgiving: 'do you forgive the bomber or gunman or knife attacker?' This has been a phenomenon in both Britain and Ireland in recent decades. It is neither fair nor an open question. There is an agenda here – one that reveals not only a lack of empathy, but also a misunderstanding of the issues which are purportedly being considered. Methodist Minister David Clements has written:

> Since Enniskillen, the right answer, the noble and worthy thing to say is 'Yes – I forgive them'. And so the widow's response is broadcast on the six o'clock news. Many commend her for her gracious words and that commendation has its short term reward. But then, as time goes by, the initial shock and numbness wear off and are replaced by anger and grief as the enormity of her irretrievable loss really sinks in and she is caught in a devilish trap. She feels anything but forgiving. Now these words spoken and broadcast earlier are like a chain around her neck.[15]

It is ridiculous, of course, to blame Gordon Wilson for this trend, but helpful to see it as a product of how his contribution is too easily simplified and misunderstood. Wilson's words were not words of forgiveness *per se* but they were words that came from a forgiving heart. Was he forgiving? Yes. Did he forgive? No. It would be impossible of course for a journalist to ask a deep question such as: 'Do you aspire to be a forgiving person and, if so, what does that require of you right now?' It is, however, the correct question. It is also, I suspect, the question that goes through the mind of every victim of shattering crime who has ever prayed the Lord's Prayer: can I still be a forgiving person?

## Lucy's sister

Marian Partington's sister, Lucy Partington, was one of the victims of Fred and Rosemary West, the serial murderers from Gloucester. Her story is one of many told in the F-Word exhibition of the Forgiveness Project.[16] She has also been interviewed by David Self as part of a larger project concerning the way in which different people struggle with forgiveness:[17]

> As soon as the news came through that Lucy's body had been found at 25 Cromwell Road, I vowed to try and bring something positive out of this meaningless trauma. But first I had to face the truth. Lucy had been abducted, gagged, raped, tortured and murdered, before she was beheaded and dismembered. For a year after the finding, her remains were needed as an exhibit for the defence. After this I felt an instinctive need to go to the mortuary in Cardiff to hold and wrap her bones. During that moving ceremony something shifted and I made a step towards peace.[18]

In her memoir *Salvaging the Sacred* she describes this experience in the mortuary. She asked if her sister's skull was inside the smaller of two cardboard boxes in the coffin. The mortician confirmed that it was and began to open the lid:

> As we drew nearer I gasped at the beauty of her skull. It was like burnished gold and it was something that was part of Lucy that had survived to tell the tale. At that moment I was full of the joy of finding something that had been part of

> Lucy after all these years. Not a glimmer of fear, not a morbid thought entered the experience. I lifted her skull with great care and tenderness and kissed her brow.[19]

Later that year, while on a Chan Buddhist retreat, she made a vow to forgive the Wests. She knew this would be a journey through uncharted territory but it also seemed the most positive way forward. The journey, however, took an unexpected turn:

> When I came home from the retreat I had an overwhelming, involuntary, and profoundly physical experience of murderous rage. It went… Whoosh! All the way up from my belly to my skull. I wanted to scream, pull my hair out, claw at the ground.[20]

When it came, Marian's delayed reaction was inevitably complicated and deep. But notice that she did not describe her full body scream as an outpouring of *grief*. It was 'an overwhelming, involuntary, and profoundly physical experience of murderous *rage*'. She goes on to say that, 'Until then I hadn't thought of myself as a murderous person, but at that moment I was capable of killing. In other words, I was not separate from the Wests.'

It sounds deeply paradoxical that a forgiveness journey should begin in an experience of 'murderous rage'. But there are several layers to this simple statement. The first, I think, is that this was her way into feeling the moral and emotional *enormity* of what had happened. As she cherished her sister's bones in her arms, she was taken to a new place in human experience. This is not merely heartache but the heart sinking to depths never previously fathomed, or even imagined. But the way she describes it means that she not only experienced this but was aware of her own response. It was this self-awareness that enabled her to connect with the Wests.

The boundaries between 'good me' and 'evil them' began to be broken down. It was in the depths of disorienting rage that she began to allow herself to identify with the very people who had mistreated and murdered her sister. It was a process that continued as Marian paid attention to Rosemary West at the trial. At first she could not connect the person in the dock with the 'endless graphic details of sexual depravities and brutality that were read out hour after hour for five days by a barrister'.[21] It was when she heard her voice as recorded in police interviews that she began to build a mental picture of Rosemary West.

> I soon got the feeling that her deviant ignorance sprang from the fact that she had rarely known beauty, truth or love. I tried to imagine growing up in an environment where fear and abuse were the main components. Her most common epithet was predictable and disturbingly accurate in the context of her world: 'bloody'.
>
> I began to understand her need to have absolute control, to cause pain and ultimately death, that she acted out in the night life at 25 Cromwell Street; the deep violent rage of impotence and ignorance that led to such terrible cruelty; the impoverishment of a soul that knew no other way to live.
>
> Her behaviour was bestial and brutal in its attempt to make her victims experience a feeling of extreme pain, humiliation and impotence.[22]

She goes on to speculate that perhaps Rosemary herself had been subjected to exactly such experiences in the past. As I read and re-read these words, I marvel at the generosity of spirit that lies behind this venture of empathy. Having accepted the heart-rending depths of her own sadness, and the reality of her rage, Marian allows her mind to drift, as it were, into the mind of the woman who was the cause of unspeakable suffering. Extraordinarily, she catches a glimpse of light:

> There was one little glimmer of insight into Rosemary West's imagination that both touched my heart and disturbed me. It was the only reference to beauty during a week full of endless statements of explicit, crude sexual detail, which were expanded upon in the recent trial. It was her attempt to lure Alison Chambers to come and live in Cromwell Street by promising her a life in the country at the weekends on 'their farm' where she would be able 'to ride horses and *write poetry*'.[23]

Marian goes on to comment: 'There was something about the use of the word "poetry" that leapt out of the general mire of blasphemy and made my stomach churn.'[24] I see more than one level in this. There is the 'click' with poetry. Lucy had spent a lot of her childhood involved in both activities and the two sisters read English at university. Lucy continued to write poetry and after her death a collection was published by her family. But there is also an insight here to the significance of the poetic in forgiveness. We have already seen that Jill Scott makes this connection in a theoretical way but in this real and ongoing story the poetic is actually and practically present. It is a subtle dimension which blends together creativity, empathy, imagination and the desire for a beauty which is both aesthetic and ethical.

In her more recent, and as yet unpublished, writing Marian talks of 'transformation'. The word is in danger of being devalued by overuse but it points to the spiritual work which she is engaged in though empathy and her poetic imagination. There is horror and sadness in Lucy's story and many will recoil from it, allowing their disgust and anger to distance them and defend them from the pain. Marian's response to her own enraged reaction was to go in the other direction, to drop the defences and seek to understand the one who is so utterly other and yet so ultimately connected. But the journey outward was also a journey inward. Before reaching out she had to reach in.

Marian's journey, since learning of the way her sister's life ended, has been complex, deep and often painful. It has progressed through a rich blending together of honesty and imagination. It has involved engaging with prisoners, spiritual practices and seeking to write about her journey and Lucy's life in such a way as might illuminate both the darkness of the reality and the depth of experience that has flowed from it. The process seems to be driven along not by any kind of direct desire to forgive but a broader sentiment that her sister's sadness, suffering and death should not be the last word.

The phrase 'salvaging the sacred' is apt for what she has been attempting while the word 'forgiveness' feels too stark. The noun itself it not dynamic or lively enough to describe what has been going on and yet, as she has recently written: 'The word "forgiving" became alive as aeons of barnacles of impossible piety that have encrusted the possible experience signified by this word with religious, pretentious dogma (especially my own) dropped away, *for*giving.'[25] This image of forgiveness itself needing to be freed is a vivid one. It suggests that it is when we manage to salvage or 'discover' or 'liberate' or 'connect with' the sacred, that forgiveness itself is liberated and forgiving begins to happen.

Marian once had a dream in which she met Rosemary West and said: 'I forgive you.' But, she writes: 'It was meaningless.' She believes that the path to forgiveness starts much closer to home:

> I'm learning how to forgive myself, and I'm learning to believe that others can forgive me. In this process I've explored my own rotting pile of mistakes, but I also see that it's my compost. It has meaning. It doesn't have to remain repulsive, something I can't acknowledge, something I want to edit out. It actually is part of who I am, and I have to develop another relationship with it.[26]

Such self-acceptance lies behind what is perhaps the most remarkable part of Marian's story. On one of her retreats she wrote a letter to Rosemary West. Four years later she posted it. In it she wrote these extraordinary words:

> At last I can tell you something that you may not understand but which may help you too in some way. I can honestly say that at times I feel a strange sort of gratitude towards you, because I have had to face myself as a human being, deep inside. Now I know a truer compassion for the terrible suffering that you have created by your actions, for yourself and for so many other people.[27]

There was no direct reply. But the story itself has not ended.

## Reflection

These two tragic stories have helped to open up some of the questions of forgiveness. In Wilson's case we have the words of a man of a forgiving disposition uttered very soon after the death of his daughter in a terrorist bomb attack in which he was himself caught up as a victim. I have suggested that we read them as more than a 'report' on his emotional disposition at the time and see them, in the context of a seemingly endless cycle of violence and reprisals, as a political message to Loyalist paramilitaries. On the other hand they do reflect his feelings: 'I was not angry then and I am not angry now.'

But these feelings, like the words, need to be treated both as a matter of character and context. The point being that the violence of the bombing, while shocking, was not a new chapter in the story of Northern Ireland. Wilson's response was not only newsworthy but 'new' in a much richer sense. It was both creative and consistent with the values of the new covenant, the religious and spiritual revolution which Jesus inaugurated as he broke the bread and shared the Passover wine as his blood was shed for the forgiveness of sins.

Wilson's words reflected his desire to make a contribution in the context of his daughter's death which did not make matters worse or fuel the culture of retaliation and revenge that was having such devastating consequences on individuals and communities. Part of their power and integrity came from the fact that he did *not* use the word forgiveness. Had he done so he would have been open to the claim that he was speaking out of turn, or pretending to an authority he did not have. As it was, he made a simple statement about his own attitude to what had happened. It was up to others to decide how they would respond but his voice of calm and integrity – a still small voice – proved to speak more powerfully than the bomb blast. What it spoke of, however, was the integrity and the power of the forgiving heart, not the power of 'forgiveness' *per se*; still less of pardon.

Wilson's words were about the subjectivity and integrity of his response. They left open the question of whether and how the bombers might be forgiven. They were not words of forgiveness nor of victim's absolution. In fact, they are better considered as prophetic words than quasi-priestly ones; words which do not announce forgiveness but which call for *repentance*. They were inviting men of violence to think and to act differently and at the same time opening up a new space, one in which forgiveness might be understood in a more generous, creative and productive way.

'I have no ill will. I bear no grudge': the words challenged the persistent and determined grudge-bearers and vengeance-seekers to adopt a new mind and attitude and to seek to try to find a new way forward. Wilson did not consciously intend them to be prophetic any more than he intended them as words of absolution. But that only adds to their power. When God speaks through the integrity of the human heart something happens that transcends human intentionality.

Had Wilson intended to speak God's word on that occasion he might well have become preachy or pious, ponderous or pompous. I say this not out of any knowledge of Wilson himself but from my observation that these are the besetting communication sins of those who would speak for God. Rather, he spoke simply and from the heart and, as it happens, his will was at that moment so closely aligned with God's that the world stopped for a moment to listen intently and wonder. Astonishingly, the words 'got through'. But these words were not pretending to have any authority or power to forgive, they were expressing the newness which is characteristic of God's spirit. They were also, in their own way, poetic. Unintentionally but realistically so, for they were words from the heart which caught the imagination.

Marian Partington's story is set in a very different time frame. Her sister had been dead for twenty years before the fact that she had been abused and murdered by the Wests was discovered, and so her grieving was at a very different stage and shrouded by much ambiguity. When she learnt of Lucy's death, the story of what had happened at the Wests' house in Gloucester was only just being discovered and so there were ambiguities there too. There was no wider political story to engage with, but it was very much in the public domain. The details were horrifying and the pain of living with uncorrected lies about her sister being told in court and repeated in the press were profoundly distressing. The reality was a domestic one of hidden cruelty and unheard screams.

What frames this as a story of forgiveness however are two things. First, her resolve, before succumbing to her overwhelming feelings of rage, to make something positive from this and second, her subsequent insight that forgiveness is not an event but something ongoing. Between the two there are other highly charged moments. Her experience of a murderous rage, the time she cradled her sister's bones, the moments in the trial when she glimpsed something of Rosemary West's mind, the retreats, the writing of a letter to Rosemary West and posting it four years later, only to receive a reply that no further letters would be passed on. This is no straightforward 'forgiveness story' and yet Partington's forgiving spirit, far from being daunted, seems stronger than ever.

The other aspect of Marian Partington's story is its creativity and carefulness. She has lived out exactly the sort of journey that Jill Scott has in mind when she talks of the poetics of forgiveness. There are several points at which this becomes evident, not least in her writing. For instance, the way she likens her sister's skull to 'burnished gold' and describes forgiveness itself as encrusted with 'aeons of barnacles of impossible piety'. Such words, and the images they inspire, not only describe reality, they begin to transform it. Martha Minow says that to try to describe things after atrocity is to fail fully to respect or appreciate them. But she adds that to keep silent does not do justice either.[28] Shattering reality calls for language that can heal and reintegrate. This, I think, is why the poetic register is so important after serious hurt or violation. The deliberate thoughtfulness manifest in the words chosen and used stimulates a different quality of relating.

As you read them you can almost hear the care with which they were chosen and articulated. The feel of the words matters; they are the right words only when they are congruent with both the pain of realty and with the generous, trusting, vulnerable empathy that is integral to forgiving.

Jill Scott has written that, 'poetic forgiveness is perhaps best understood as a function of writing, reading and reflection, arising in the form and medium of texts and in the melodies and rhythms of language itself'.[29] It sounds fanciful, but it is not. Forgiving is absolutely about refusing to take harsh and ugly events, perceptions and descriptions on their own terms. It is a matter of moving things to a higher register. It is not merely about declining to engage in revenge, letting go of resentment or accepting apology. It is about the triumph of *grace*. And the creative, concrete and poetic use of words is nothing less than the spiritual effort to allow grace to speak. Victims do not need a theory of forgiveness that they might implement. They need a story of forgiveness and the poetic confidence to write themselves into its plot.

Neither Wilson nor Partington claim to have forgiven those responsible for the murder of Marie or Lucy and yet these are both stories where we can see a forgiving spirit in action, where we see the way in which a forgiving heart beats in the aftermath of murder. They are very different stories but in both we see generosity of spirit, creativity and integrity. Neither Wilson nor Partington followed any kind of rule-book or process in what they did (or in Partington's case 'do' – her story is not yet over.) Their 'method' was to take one step at a time, let the heart make one beat at a time, and see where that led them. In this way they are explorers taking risks with an integrity which is not content to let evil or death, bitterness or hatred, have the last word. They move forward at a pace driven by external events: for Wilson it was very fast, for Partington it is very slow, and yet they meet those events with the creativity, hope and generous empathy which are hallmarks of the forgiving heart.

## Notes

1. Various news reports, 30 November 2005, http://news.bbc.co.uk/1/hi/england/merseyside/4471440.stm.
2. Wilson, G. and McCreary, A. *Marie*, p. xiv.
3. Wilson, G. and McCreary, A. *Marie*, p. xiii.
4. Garrard, E. and McNaughton, D. *Forgiveness*, p. 1.
5. Wilson, G. and McCreary, A. *Marie*, p. 92.
6. Bolton, N. 'The Transformational Possibilities of Forgiveness' in Spencer G *Forgiving and Remembering in Northern Ireland*, p. 211. Bolton refers to Bardon's *A History of Ulster* (Belfast: Blackstaff Press, 1992) as supporting this view.
7. Quoted by Alwyn Thompson in 'Forgiveness and the Political Process in Northern Ireland' in McFadyen, A. and Sarot, M. (eds) *Forgiveness and Truth*, pp. 140–141.
8. Kinahan, T. in Spencer, G. (ed.) *Forgiving and Remembering in Northern Ireland*, p. 80.
9. Spencer, G. (ed.) *Forgiving and Remembering in Northern Ireland*, p. 214.
10. Spencer, G. (ed.) *Forgiving and Remembering in Northern Ireland*, p. 245.
11. Wilson, G. and McCreary, A. *Marie*, p. 93.
12. Wilson, G. and McCreary, A. *Marie*, p. 92.
13. Wilson, G. and McCreary, A. *Marie*, p. 92.
14. Wilson, G. and McCreary, A. *Marie*, p. 91.
15. Spencer, G. (ed.) *Forgiving and Remembering in Northern Ireland*, p. 243.
16. The best way to access *The Forgiveness Project* is through the website: http://theforgivenessproject.org.uk.
17. Self, D. 'Enfolding the Dark' in McFadyen, A. and Sarot, M. (eds) *Forgiveness and Truth* also Self, D. *Struggling with Forgiveness.*
18. http://theforgivenessproject.com/stories/marian-partington-england/.
19. Partington, M. *Salvaging the Sacred*, p. 16.
20. http://theforgivenessproject.com/stories/marian-partington-england/.
21. Partington, M. *Salvaging the Sacred*, p. 19.
22. Partington, M. *Salvaging the Sacred*, p. 20.
23. Partington, M. *Salvaging the Sacred*, p. 21.

24. Partington, M. *Salvaging the Sacred*, p. 21.
25. Partington, M. *If You Sit Very Still* (in press).
26. Self, D. *Struggling with Forgiveness*, p. 20.
27. Partington, M. *If You Sit Very Still* (in press).
28. Thinking of large-scale atrocities she writes: 'Even to speak, to grope for words to describe horrific events, is to pretend to negate their unspeakable qualities and effects. Yet silence is also an unacceptable offence, a shocking implication that the perpetrators in fact succeeded, a stunning indictment that the present audience is simply the current incarnation of the silent bystanders complicit with oppressive regimes.' Minow, M. *Between Vengeance and Forgiveness*, p. 5.
29. Scott, J. *A Poetics of Forgiveness*, p. 199.

## CHAPTER 7

# Forgiveness as Spirituality

In Chapter 4 we examined Jesus' teaching on forgiveness in some detail and concluded that his followers should actively seek to develop a forgiving heart. However, although forgiveness is integral to the life of Christian discipleship, it is not the solution to every problem between people and, at the human level, forgiveness is not always possible. Learning how to live as a follower of Jesus involves developing a forgiving spirit, a forgiving heart. But what of Jesus' own life and actions? Was Jesus a forgiving person? The question might sound outrageous but it is both more important and more difficult to answer than might be supposed.

The standard story about forgiveness is that people are offended or injured, have a justified but negative emotional response and then let go of that response, together with any hostile attitude towards the perpetrator. When such a process has happened people speak of having forgiven or having been forgiven. There is, however, a distinct lack of evidence in the gospels that this process of human forgiveness happened in or around Jesus in advance of his crucifixion. He was involved in plenty of controversy, he spoke many harsh words and was sometimes threatened and attacked, but these incidents are all unresolved. The gospel writers seem to be entirely uninterested in the relational consequences of the brief encounters they record. As an itinerant preacher, healer and

Rabbi, Jesus did not present as a particularly forgiving person. He was a man on a mission, a prophet. Certainly he had a compassionate heart, but his compassion was very much for the poor and suffering and as far removed from an easy tolerance as his urgency and pace of life were different to measured patience. Jesus was a passionate and energetic preacher of repentance and the coming of the kingdom. He reached out to the sick with healing. He told the poor that they are of supreme spiritual value, and that God's kingdom is in a profound sense 'for' them. However, we see very little of personal forgiveness in the life and ministry of Jesus before his passion.

## The Agony

Early in my ministry I had the task of supporting a man who was dying of cancer through his last weeks. On one occasion he looked up after having said the Lord's Prayer and said: 'That's the hardest bit, the hardest prayer.' I looked a little puzzled so he answered simply: '"Thy will be done", those are the most difficult words.' Anyone reading the story of Jesus in the garden of Gethsemane would come to the same conclusion.

It is possible to see the struggle in the garden as the process whereby Jesus sought to reconcile himself to the pain and death of crucifixion – 'let this cup [of suffering] pass from me'. That is to focus on the fear of pain and death and to see the drops of sweated blood as symptomatic of terror. But there is another way too, which focuses on the second half of the prayer 'not my will but your will be done' and sees the agony of the garden as precisely the struggle to reconcile the independence of the human will with the other-centred, forgiving and loving purposes of the divine will. Jesus was, as theologians have long since established, fully human and fully divine. What we see in the garden is the intensification of a tension that all human beings know – the agonizing tension between the will of God and our own personal will. Here Jesus is taken to the agony implicit in the prayer he had taught his disciples: 'Thy will be done.'

I say this not to seek to minimize the fear of anticipated crucifixion but because it is possible to underplay the psychological aspects of what happens to human beings under stress. In *The Railway Man*, Eric Lomax emphasized that while the physical scars and symptoms of torture do go away after a while, the psychological scars remain. The psychology of Jesus' situation is complex indeed and the fear of pain and death is clearly part of it. But added to the mix is also the expected betrayal, the anticipated shame and the actual agony of discerning and following the will of God. The will and desire of God was clearly in Jesus' mind and yet there remained a distance between Jesus' will and God's will. While Jesus' mission can be understood as an expression of his desire to share the human condition, we can imaginatively share in his condition in the garden, because it is so precisely ours when we are both at our most agonized and at our best. That is, when we are struggling with God's will.

The agony in the garden can be for us an icon of repentance. It is a picture through which we can see what is involved in accommodating our own will to that of God. One thing this makes abundantly clear is that repentance is struggle. The repentance that opens for us God's forgiveness is our reorientation to the will of God and away from our own ego-desires. Herbert McCabe makes this clear when he writes that God's forgiveness of us *is* our repentance; that God's forgiveness is not a change in God but in us:

> We speak of God forgiving not because he really is offended but accepts our apology or agrees to overlook the insult. What God is doing is like forgiveness not because of anything that happens in God, but because of what happens in us, because of the *re-creative* and *redemptive* side of forgiveness. All the insult and injury we do in sinning is to ourselves alone, not to God. We speak of God forgiving us because he comes to save us from ourselves, to restore us after we have injured ourselves, to redeem and re-create us.[1]

There is no extra work to be done on our part after repentance in order to be able to avail ourselves of God's forgiveness. Accepting God's will, engaging wholeheartedly in God's mission and purposes *are* our repentance and our forgiveness. Gethsemane gives us a clear indication that this only happens through the most profound soul searching and with spiritual courage and resolve. Jesus does not repent or seek forgiveness as we do, but his agony in the garden is nonetheless an indication of the nature of the struggle that any human being might have in accommodating to the will of God.

Jesus' intuition told him that this was not a struggle he should embark on alone and so he took his three trusted companions; the same three, Peter, James and John, who had climbed the mountain of transfiguration. But on this occasion they were disappointing. As Jesus struggled and prayed they slept. There is a powerful message for contemporary disciples in this behaviour for it reminds us that deep down we do not want to know; we neither want to witness nor share in struggles like this. Just as Jesus enters into the heart of spirituality, that battle to the death between the will of God and the will of self, so the disciples lose the energy and the will to be party to it.

Once again we must not read the story simply in terms of the physical side. That they were tired and slept does not only mean that they were physically exhausted, it also means that they were content to avoid the issue and to hold on to the happy memories of their time together on the road: the healing and the teaching, the adventures and arguments, the triumphal entry, the fracas in the temple and the happy fellowship of their intimate Passover.

That was the fun of discipleship, and yes, they were learning and growing all the while. But now things have changed. Jesus is taking another step; he has moved, suddenly, to a different place, a rugged territory where the self must go head to head with the divine will. There's no fun in that, only struggle and death. It seems much more important to catch up on a few minutes' sleep and let the wine wear off. It is going to be a long night anyway and strength will be needed in the morning. They are right in that, but they are not right in the assumptions that they make about strength. True strength comes not from preparing for the morning by sleep but from engaging in the agony of the moment. Jesus is all but defeated in prayer and yet emerges strong. They sleep peacefully and yet are shown to be inadequate to the challenge of continuing as disciples.

So the disciples manage to avoid the agony of the garden, the aguish of wrestling with the divine will which seeks not to destroy the self but to integrate and align it in such a way that will make for a community of love and joy and peace. Jesus struggles alone but his struggle is not unique. That struggle lies at the heart of all discipleship. Whereas his death is once and for all in opening the way to resurrection, the agony in the garden is an enduring icon of repentance. No one sleeps while Jesus is on the *cross*. Golgotha compels our attention. It is Gethsemane that makes our eyelids droop, and yet it is here that the healing agony is at it most spiritually intense and creative.

Jesus emerges from the garden integrated within himself and reconciled with God and it is with the power of the internal at-one-ness, or integration, that he stands before Pilate and Herod, mystifying and bewildering them because he is on a different wavelength from their self-interested fascination with power and amusement. Indeed he so puzzles and alienates them that they are reconciled from that day on.[2] A reminder, perhaps, that not all reconciliation is good. It is reconciliation with the will of God that is good and which is indistinguishable from both repentance and forgiveness.

Gethsemane is in some ways darker and more dangerous than even the cross. It is the internal agony, the wrestling with my will versus God's will, the negotiation of the claims of fantasy and reality, the need not for submission so much as acceptance and ownership which make this so deeply troubling and unattractive. We can no more bear it than can the disciples because we know in the depths of our hearts that this struggle is not Jesus' alone – it is also ours. He can die for us, but he cannot do for us that one thing that we need to do for ourselves which is to die to ourselves. Jesus in the garden terrifies us because we know that before we can even carry a cross we first have to enter into that struggle which caused Jacob to limp and Jesus to sweat blood: the struggle with the will of God. It is the struggle that lies behind all forgiving.

## The Cross

The first indication that we see of Jesus engaging in forgiveness of others on his own behalf, rather than indirectly through teaching or alongside healing, is when he is dying on the cross.

The words are found in Luke's gospel only: 'Then Jesus said, "Father forgive them; for they know not what they are doing"' (Luke 23.34). They also come with a warning in the footnotes: apparently, this verse is lacking 'in many ancient authorities'.

When we first begin to think about it, that is quite an uncomfortable thought. Suppose Jesus did *not* offer forgiveness from the cross? What then of our idea that forgiveness is at the heart of Christian teaching, faith and life? We can take some comfort from the thought that even if these words were added later they are there for a reason. Maybe there was a folk memory about these words that Luke, like the other evangelists, did not get to hear, or simply forgot. Or perhaps it became clear to the early followers of Jesus that even if no one could say for sure, then this was just the sort of thing that Jesus would have said.

The words reveal his character, his heart, and so are true to him and his message, though this might be something that became more evident in retrospect than it was in the days when Jesus' record as a somewhat irascible itinerant preacher was fresher in people's minds. By the time the church had come to define itself as the community which was held together by the memory of Jesus' death and resurrection, re-enacted in baptism and Eucharist, the message of forgiveness would have become more predominant, despite the fact that there was so little evidence of interpersonal forgiveness in the gospel stories.

On the other hand, there is an emphasis on human forgiveness and interpersonal reconciliation in the post-Easter resurrection stories and these words can be seen in that light. They show the overlap between the healing ministry of Jesus as described before the passion and the mission which is revealed in the resurrection stories. The prayer for forgiveness lies at the heart of the ministry and mission of Jesus but when uttered from the cross it comes from the heart of his being. These are the most extreme conditions of physical pain and psychological alienation but also of public exposure and vulnerability and it raises this question: what does a person with a forgiving heart do under extreme conditions?

Luke's account of the crucifixion of Jesus does not have the physical horror of Mark or Matthew and it spares us the cry of desolation and abandonment. Jesus is not forsaken in Luke's calm story. However, if we attend to it carefully, the account reveals the horrors of cruelty and humiliation: two chilling realities which can inflict devastating harm without leaving so much as a bruise, for they come not necessarily with blows but with attitudes, gestures and sneering words. Luke's version of the crucifixion is a story not primarily of physical but of psychological cruelty.

The two come together, of course, but it is the psychological aspect that takes Jesus to the place where, if there is to be any kind of positive fellow feeling – never mind love of neighbour or enemy – it is going to have to take the form of *extreme forgiveness*. No wonder the daughters of Jerusalem who are present weep and beat their breasts; no wonder those who walk away afterwards do the same; no wonder the centurion recognizes that this man was innocent. For the one who prays for forgiveness is the one who has been betrayed and disowned, is the one who has been subject to derision and mockery – scoffing – from people of successively diminishing status: the leaders, the Romans and then an executed criminal. Jesus' prayer for forgiveness comes from one who is both reconciled to himself and to God and yet alienated by others who energetically engage in his humiliating destruction.

Jesus' prayer for their forgiveness is an example, perhaps *the* definitive example, of extreme forgiveness and I make this point because what Jesus is doing by uttering this prayer from the cross is not completing a nice, formulaic forgiveness process but addressing the consequences of human sinfulness and evil. Jesus forgives and dies at the Place of the Skull: a hard, dry and desperate place. Every attempt possible has been made to break his spirit, his passionate, loving, healing, forgiving spirit. He will soon die, a relief to be sure, but there is, I believe, the first flicker of the paschal candle, the first glimpse of Pentecostal wind and flame in that almost unheard prayer, 'Father, forgive them'. A prayer which matches, balances and completes the Gethsemane prayer 'thy will be done'. It is these prayers said together which open up the path to the new life in Christ that is resurrection and eternal life.

'My task is to seek to do your will; my prayer is that you forgive those who hurt me for doing it.' These are the two complementary beats of the broken heart of Christ and they can be echoed in the depths of those who learn how to live and die with him. But notice that what we have been discussing here is not a statement or announcement or promise of forgiveness but a *prayer for forgiveness*. Prayer is the language of the heart under pressure. True forgiveness rarely takes the form 'forgiven' and yet even more rarely 'I have forgiven'. True forgiveness, like true prayer, is aspiration, struggle and openness to the will and love of God. It is from this mix, which is appropriately called 'spirituality', that new life is born. And in this new life the receiving and the giving of forgiveness are like the inhalation and exhalation of breath. They are the flow of the Spirit.

## Resurrection

The clearest and most complete example of a forgiveness story in the Gospels takes place after the resurrection of Jesus on the seashore just after breakfast (John 21.1-19). Jesus had done the cooking and his guests were Peter, Thomas, Nathanael and a few others. We note in passing that the breakfast was prepared on a charcoal fire. As we know, charcoal fires have a distinctive smell and while for us it might mean a warm evening and a cool beer with friends at a barbeque, for Peter the smell evoked something very different. For it was while he was warming himself at another charcoal fire that he had had a very different and shaming conversation a few days previously; the conversation in which he had denied Jesus three times (John 18.15-27).

Jesus asks Peter three questions. In fact, that is not quite right, he asks him two versions of the same question a total of three times (John 21.15-19): 'Simon, son of John, do you love me more than these?' Most translations of the Bible obscure the fact that two different words are both translated 'love' here. In the first two questions Jesus asks: 'Do you love me?[3] In the reply, however, Peter says: 'You know that I am your friend.'[4] In the third question Jesus changes his word and asks: 'Are you my friend?'[5] It is after this third time, when Jesus uses Peter's own word, that Peter is 'grieved' and says: 'You know everything; you know that I am your friend,' resenting, perhaps, that he needs to affirm what he has already said twice.

What is Jesus' response to this confession of friendship or fondness? Not words of forgiveness but words of commission. He gives Peter responsibility three times: 'feed my lambs', 'tend my sheep', 'feed my sheep'. Then he tells him that he too will come to a cruel death and then, just to seal the point about both sacrifice and discipleship, he says: 'Follow me.'

Now *that* is a forgiveness story. Like Jesus at the wedding in Cana, John has served the best wine last (John 2.1-11) for this is the wine of new life based on trust and empowerment. Jesus may not have spoken the words, 'I forgive you' to Peter, but he has certainly forgiven him. He has restored him to his calling as a disciple and given him the ways and means he needs to deliver on the leadership commission that he was given when he was first called Peter, 'you are Peter, and on this rock I will build my church' (Matthew 16.18). He has underlined three times not the authority of power, or the mission of the leader, but the fundamental duty: to nourish and nurture, to feed and to tend.

This is a transformational encounter in which the burden of shortcomings in the past is removed and there is the gift of new responsibility, role and relationship. This refection on the encounter between Jesus and Peter suggests that it holds together the two sides of forgiveness that make up the New Testament picture of forgiveness, the graceful giving (*charizomai*) and the releasing (*apheimi*).

It is often remarked that John's gospel begins by consciously paralleling the opening words of the book of Genesis: 'In the beginning' (Genesis 1.1 and John 1.1). Reading this commissioning of Peter as a forgiveness story suggests another parallel with Genesis. For Genesis also has a defining story of forgiveness as it comes to its conclusion when Joseph forgives his brothers with great subtlety and tact (Genesis 50.15-21).[6] Both Genesis and John end with stories of human or interpersonal forgiveness: Joseph of his brothers, Jesus of Peter. The burden of the past is removed and the possibility of a new future given. Both books begin at the beginning and end with the new beginning that we call forgiveness.

## The Last Supper

At the Last Supper, Jesus takes, breaks and blesses the bread and shares it with his companions as 'my body given *for* you'. Later, he takes a cup of wine and asks them to drink of it as his blood – 'poured out *for* the forgiveness of sins'. In order to make sense of this we need to remember the root meaning of forgiveness in the Greek word *aphesis*: releasing, freeing from that which constrains. We also need to appreciate that when Jesus says that the wine is his blood, he is inviting us to see it as life-giving.

Luke's story of the disciples on the road to Emmaus has often been identified as having a life-giving shape (Luke 24.13-35). First, the stranger explains the scriptures and blesses and breaks the bread. He (Jesus) does not instantly reveal himself or immediately offer instruction or demand that the disciples repent. The mode of engagement, rather, is to accompany the two frightened and disillusioned disciples as they walk *away* from Jerusalem, as they progress in the wrong direction. Jesus walks with them and listens to them. As the conversation unfolds there is an element of rebuke and forthright challenge but nothing like the fierce instructions to repent that we find in either the prophets of old, or in John the Baptist, or in the first phase of Jesus' ministry.

The forlorn disciples *do* repent when they at last see what is revealed in the breaking of the bread. That is, they turn around and they quickly embark on a new journey, this time in the right direction. They go back to Jerusalem, the holy city. But even more significantly, the journey is back to the company of the other disciples, those whom they had deserted. They are welcomed back with news that the Lord had risen and appeared to Simon (Luke 24.34) and the eleven and their companions all listen intently to the story of what happened on the road.

The pattern of blessing, breaking and sharing persists in the continued remembrance of the Last Supper which Christians call Eucharist (a Greek word which means 'thanksgiving') or Mass. It encapsulates and passes on a specific understanding of a relationship with God that is based on a new kind of forgiveness. This new forgiveness addresses the reality that fear and confusion contribute to the tragic self-imprisonment of human beings which is reflected in the effort to journey away from God. Seeing that we are incapable of resolving this issue, God in Christ offers us a connection with the divine life by inviting us to share in his identity by receiving the bread and wine which he calls his body and blood. What matters above all else here is that this identity is itself already formed though a process of reaching out beyond itself to the lives of others.

The Last Super is a celebration of forgiveness which invites repentance. But the repentance which it invites is only partially understood as a reorientation towards God. As it is a sharing in the body and blood of *Christ*, who has often been called the 'man *for* others', it is also a reorientation towards neighbour. That neighbour is not only a loved one but also a feared one, a resented one or a hated one. Jesus transforms our understanding of forgiveness from something we might receive when we repent, to something God offers but which we need help to receive.

He also changes our understanding of repentance from a reorientation to God to a reorientation towards 'those who have sinned against us' and so it is that Jesus gives us a gift which requires not that we reorient ourselves us to God in acts of other-worldly piety or ritualized religiosity, but that we become people who are *for* others. That 'for-other-ness' is the basis of 'for-give-ness' for what we have to give is nothing more or less than what we have been given. As the Reverend John Ames says in Marilynne Robinson's novel *Gilead* when he summarizes the conclusion of a sermon he once preached on the story of the prodigal son:

> It says Jesus puts His hearer in the role of the father, of those who forgive. Because if we are, so to speak the debtor (and

> of course we are that, too), that suggests no graciousness in us. And grace is the great gift. So to be forgiven is only half the gift. The other half is that we also can forgive, restore, and liberate, and therefore we can feel the will of God enacted through us which is the great restoration of ourselves to ourselves.[7]

As we shall see in a subsequent chapter, it is possible to overdo this identification with the father and see ourselves as aloof, or as those who are sinned against. The parable only works for us spiritually if we allow ourselves to identify with the two younger men as well, both the prodigal son and the grudging brother. But none of this undermines the fundamental point that forgiveness is offered to us *before* we deserve it and that our repentance involves adopting a forgiving attitude to our neighbours. What this suggests is that there is a dynamic flow of grace to others through ourselves, and to ourselves from others. In this sense, all human beings are fundamentally called to be *for* giving and *for* others.

A similar twist happens in the gospels regarding the meaning and importance of baptism. John the Baptizer preaches a 'baptism of repentance' and we can see how this stands in the prophetic tradition which invites us to approach the forgiving God by turning to a life more in line with God's values and nature, and less preoccupied with self-interest. In other passages, baptism is connected with forgiveness. The baptism is not an initiation into a process of trying to repent but is a more literal washing away of, or freeing from, sin and its consequences. In baptism, we see that forgiving is what God does. God's concern and care for sinners takes the risky first step to support the sinful soul *before* it has yet repented. Freed from the burden of seeking forgiveness the baptized person has the task of seeking to live a life of repentance which involves finding authentic ways to forgive others.

## Reflection

Looking at the last supper, the agony in the garden and some of Jesus words from the cross from the perspective of forgiveness has been very instructive. Although Jesus did not actually forgive those who had wronged him in his earthly life, the dynamics of forgiveness characterize both his risen life and those aspects of his final days in which the power of resurrection begins to be become apparent: in particular in establishing the new Passover of the Eucharist and in offering the prayer for forgiveness from the cross. Nowhere do we see the giving of forgiveness as the enacting of a kind of power from an authority figure.

Even from the cross, Jesus does not evoke the 'authority of the victim' and forgive in his own name. What seems to be unfolding is a new dynamic in which the possibility of a new life is imagined, where there is a different kind of relationship with God and new quality of fellowship among people which is based on the continual reality of sin and hurt and the new healing dynamic of forgiveness: the for-other-ness of the forgiving heart.

The agony in the garden of Gethsemane reveals, however, that for human beings it is immensely difficult to achieve that integration of self and accommodation to the will of God that is both true repentance and real forgiveness. This teaches us something of how Jesus became the forgiver that he ultimately was. It also suggests why the death of the self is at the heart of Christian spirituality. It is so that the self might live integrated and whole and reconciled with the loving, yet terrifying, will of God; the will in which ultimate forgiveness is found. We become ourselves (or in the Reverend Ames words 'are restored to ourselves') when our self becomes the place through which the spirit or grace of God flows. This is the ultimate form of hospitality and generosity and it reflects precisely the for-otherness and for-giving-ness of God in Christ.

If the teaching of Jesus has told us that the vital thing is to have a forgiving heart, the practice and passion of Jesus have told us something about the nature of that heart and how it is formed. This all takes forgiveness way beyond the realm of mild tolerance, powerful speech or grandiloquent condescension. It *is* healing agony, something which we can easily lose sight of when we become too earnest in seeking to forgive or in our efforts to persuade others to do so. Issues we will explore in the next chapter.

## Notes

1. McCabe, H. *God, Christ and Us*, pp. 121–122 (original emphasis).
2. 'That same day Herod and Pilate became friends with each other; before this they had been enemies' Luke 23.12. I once heard a theologian, rather irritated by hearing endless glib clichés about Jesus as a reconciler and fearing that this was distorting Jesus' commitment to truth and justice, make the point that 'the only people Jesus ever reconciled were Pilate and Herod'. It is a point worth remembering when thinking about Jesus and forgiveness.
3. The Greek word used here is *agapas* and so properly translated 'love': 'do you love me?'
4. The Greek word used is *philo* and so a literal translation might be 'you know that I am fond (*philo*) of you'.
5. Again, the Greek word used is *philo* and so a literal translation might be 'are you fond (*philo*) of me?'
6. Jonathan Sacks argues that this passage establishes that forgiveness between people is a 'first principle' of Judaism. He goes on to say: 'Once the Torah has established the principle of human forgiveness, which it does here in

the Joseph narrative, it does not need to repeat it elsewhere.' In this way he seeks to challenge the widespread misconception that interpersonal forgiveness is foreign to Judaism. Sacks, J. *Covenant and Conversation*, p. 325.

7. Robinson, M. *Gilead*, pp. 183–184.

## CHAPTER 8

# Forgiver Syndrome

Although the Christian gospels seem to carry the message that people must forgive others if they themselves hope to be forgiven by God, we have not been convinced that this simply means that whatever someone else has done to you in the past, and whatever their attitude towards you today, you must fully forgive them. The situation is far more complex than that. For instance, there are various levels of harm and meanings for 'forgive' to be taken into account. However, this does not detract from the truth that there is, within what one might call the 'Christianity package', an ethical bias in favour of forgiving.

And yet to suggest that Christian people are expected to be careful about whom they forgive and that in difficult or dubious cases they should be advised to err on the side of not forgiving someone is surely mistaken. Christianity is, without doubt, a pro-forgiveness religion. It believes not merely in a forgiving God but that human beings should be forgiving too, that they should have a forgiving heart. We have seen that the duty to forgive is a subtle matter. In this chapter we examine with equal care the desire to forgive.

## Forgiveness Boosterism

One problem with believing that we have a duty to forgive is that it can make us forgive too easily. This might already sound like an unchristian thing to say. Certainly an Amish reader would not be comfortable with the suggestion, yet as we have seen, people often confuse forgiving with forgetting, condoning, excusing and tolerating (and continuing to tolerate) things which are not just, helpful or appropriate. In doing so, they not only make life a misery for themselves but they fail in their duty of loving a neighbour who needs to be challenged to be more respectful and considerate or maybe less selfish and aggressive. So, one problem with the desire to forgive is that it can push us in the direction of being too inclined to tolerate or to ignore injustice when we ourselves are the victims.

A deep desire to forgive can also make people too forgiving in a more specific and accurate sense of the word. We have already explored the concept of the good grudge. This is the attenuated form of hostility one feels towards those responsible for an ongoing harmful and unjust situation. My argument is that this can be a form of forgiving and if that is accepted at least within a wide-angle view of forgiveness then that is fine. Nonetheless there are subtle judgements to be made and there is always a danger that the person who feels that they have a duty to forgive will be inclined to be too accepting of injustice over the long haul; that they will fail to establish the delicate dynamic balance between the demands of justice and mercy. That is, under pressure to 'forgive' (whether that is internal or external pressure) they will not be able to recognize the importance of a good grudge, which is persistent but controlled resentment against the ongoing abuse of power by those whose position is unassailable. To put it differently, they might throw out the baby of appropriate resentment with the bathwater of hate.

A pro-forgiveness culture which sees forgiveness as a moral and spiritual duty can have the effect of making people feel that they should seek to eradicate all negative feelings and ill will towards someone who is harming them and others when this is not, in fact, the best thing to do. The sort of situations I am thinking of here are not those where a one-off injury has been inflicted in the past and the victim has almost entirely recovered from it, but those where hurt, abuse or oppression is ongoing. Another danger is that people may be made to feel guilty for failing to forgive in situations where forgiveness is inappropriate. This is clearly a very unfortunate situation to arrive at: where people feel guilty for doing the right thing. Too much pressure to forgive can make life even more unpleasant for a victim.

Jeffrie Murphy coined the phrase 'forgiveness boosterism' to refer to the way in which forgiveness has been adopted as a technique and an imperative within psychotherapy. Murphy is concerned about forgiveness which is promoted as hasty, universally relevant or which, and this is his main point, fails to recognize the legitimacy of resentment.[1] Others have picked up on the term and included it in their philosophical arguments about forgiveness. Eve Garrard and David McNaughton, for instance, repeatedly refer to 'cheap boosterism' which they describe as:

> ... the pretence that it's [forgiveness is] a ready solution to the ills produced by wrongdoing, that it's easily available to all who want to cure those ills, and also that it's morally unassailable, that there are no moral reasons against it, in all circumstances.[2]

Thomas Brudholm takes a slightly different approach and focuses less on the connection between this boosterism and 'therapeutic forgiveness' and more on the cultural and political dynamics. He singles out Desmond Tutu as one who has used his position in public life to promote (or 'boost') forgiveness and to put pressure on victims to forgive in ways that are not only unhelpful but counter-productive.[3]

Brudholm is thinking of Tutu's role as chair of the South African Truth and Reconciliation Commission (TRC). It is undoubtedly true that the TRC created an environment which encouraged reconciliation in ways that were both significantly informed by Christian theology and ethics, in particular ideas about forgiveness. But at the same time there was a lack of philosophical precision about what exactly was meant by forgiveness. At an intellectual level, part of the problem was with the way in which the concepts 'truth' and 'reconciliation' were put together in the process.

One of the main slogans at the time was that 'truth is the road that leads to reconciliation'. This statement is not above question and in fact only really makes sense if certain kinds of truth are revealed and then heard and responded to by people with certain attitudes and dispositions. It is not unrealistic to see this statement as a watered down and slightly secularized version of what one might call a Christian or even Judeo Christian view that *repentance* is the road to forgiveness. It is, however, much more difficult to draw a concept like repentance into the political realm. A slogan like 'repentance is the road to reconciliation' is accurate, but of little or no political value. It is impossible to imagine it as part of a process of transitional justice or national reconstruction.

Truth does matter, of course. It is a necessary precondition for forgiveness, but also for repentance. Truth without repentance might lead to forgiveness, it has a greater chance than does falsehood, but only if it encounters a 'forgiving heart'. Tutu knew this, and as a Christian theologian, pastor and teacher, was committed to encouraging others to have such a heart. Because it is so integral to his values, and so relevant at this stage in history, he also praised forgiveness whenever it was manifest. At one level there is nothing problematic with this; good and healthy forgiveness is praiseworthy. But problems can arise. Forgiveness, as we have seen, is not clear-cut or without its ambiguities.

There are two ways of identifying the fundamental problem here. Thomas Brudolm's view is that the TRC combined two conditions which, independently, can lead to the advocacy of forgiveness becoming harmful in itself or leading to a failure adequately to respect victims who do not express forgiveness. They are, first, the extent to which forgiveness is a 'blurred' concept and, second, the degree to which forgiveness tends towards a 'maximalist' approach. By 'maximalist' Brudholm means that forgiveness is not simply in the gift of the primary victim but that all who are harmed by an unjust actions, whether directly or indirectly, might be seen as forgiving the offender.

The blurring of definition meant that in this context the word 'forgiveness' came to mean both the overcoming of vengeance *and* the willingness to accept amnesty. This, he argues, represents a failure to respect that a person might overcome resentment and at the same time insist that criminals should be punished. Or, we might add, that a person might begin to entertain the possibility of letting go of resentment only after the one who had harmed them was safely locked away. He argues that the TRC brought together both factors. '*The TRC discourse was both blurred and maximalist – and thus a preeminent example of forgiveness boosterism.*'[4]

Focussing on 'maximalism', he is critical of Tutu's encouragement of unconditional or unilateral forgiveness:

> Tutu tried to encourage the victims to take 'the first step': to articulate a willingness to forgive before even knowing whom

> to forgive and before knowing anything about the perpetrators' present attitude to their past criminal records.[5]

In other words, people were pressurized into 'forgiving' prematurely. It would be a difficult accusation to disprove. There was definitely a bias towards forgiving written into the process. For instance, one of the main South African languages is Xhosa and in that language the word used in the title of the commission can just as appropriately translate 'forgiveness' as reconciliation. So it is reasonable to suppose that many who participated would have understood themselves to be part of a *Truth and Forgiveness Commission*. Whether or not they 'forgave' in that context was not entirely relevant to the outcome of the process – for instance the granting of amnesty.

However, the TRC was never a process with only one aim in a straightforward and settled social and political context. It was an experiment in transitional justice which was informed both by Christian theology and therapeutic psychology. As such it was inevitably messy and multidimensional. There were good moments and not so good moments. It developed both admirable and less admirable practices. Brudholm is right to suggest that some of the worse moments were precipitated by a failure to make clear distinctions and an enthusiasm for expressions of generosity of spirit and *ubuntu*, and these would include public statements of forgiveness.

At the time, people felt that they were living through a kind of social and political miracle, and it is in this context that magnanimous and surprising words of forgiveness were themselves understood as miraculous, as evidence that there was more to this than an ordinary political process, that there was a transcendent or gracious element to it; that God was somehow at work.

It is wrong, however, to come to the conclusion that the reconciliation process in South Africa was dominated by such theology or that the TRC was compromised by an excessive enthusiasm for oversimplified forgiveness. I suspect, though, that while there was sometimes some pressure to forgive in a public and maybe performative way, there was less manipulation than its more severe critics suggest. But I also suspect that there was less forgiveness than is sometimes suggested or popularly imagined. Furthermore I suspect that some of the situations where it seemed as if there was no forgiveness may yet unfold in such a way that forgiveness begins to emerge.

I think, for instance, of a man who was given amnesty for four murders he was involved in. He was granted the amnesty and then sought forgiveness from the widows. Three said: 'Yes, I forgive you.' One simply slapped his face. When I encountered him he was continuing to support her. There was clearly regret on his part and in the aftermath of the slap there was ongoing restitution and ongoing relationship. Who knows how that might unfold? There is no one story, no one process running through the TRC any more than there is one ideal or normative forgiveness method in human affairs.[6]

An example of a response to being made a victim which shows a mature and sophisticated understanding of the subtleties of forgiveness is found in the story of Fr Michael Lapsley. In the years before the end of apartheid Lapsley, a priest from South Africa, was sent a letter bomb that, when it exploded, blew off his hands, burst his eardrums and blinded him in one eye. One of the many things that I find impressive about him is his reticence about forgiveness despite the fact that he describes the harm that he suffered as having made him a better priest. In fact, he is on record as saying that he cannot forgive those who bombed him, 'because I don't know who they are'. He goes on to say that even if they identified themselves, confessed and were full of sorrow it would not be right to let them walk free. They should at least take responsibility for all the extra help he needs just to get through daily life.[7]

Lapsley adds an important dimension to the discussion here. When people carry deliberately inflicted wounds and scars, internal and external, the responsibility of the perpetrator for their ongoing suffering and incapacity cannot be dismissed with a few kind words offered in delighted response to an expression of regret. The desire to forgive and to be seen to be a forgiving person itself needs to be handled with care, and sometimes with restraint. Such an attitude of 'restrained forgivingness' is a vital corrective to what we might call 'heroic forgiveness' which might offer a performance of condescending virtue which is more about the pride of the forgiver than the healing of the perpetrator.

Lapsley's approach is informed by straightforward humility and realism. He knows that his relationship with his bombers cannot progress until they come forward or he knows who they are; and if he knew who they were, he would no doubt also be interested in their feelings about what they had done to him. If Lapsley wanted to 'play God', he might have made grand gestures and speeches about having forgiven his bombers. Some in his situation might derive comfort from doing so. But as someone who has to live with no hands, and all the other consequences of being attacked as he was, he is very much in touch with the pain of the human condition. He has no reason to pretend to rise above it.[8]

There is no doubt that Tutu is an advocate of forgiveness, partly on therapeutic grounds. His views are famous: 'It is good for you', 'it is the highest form of self-interest', 'there is no future without forgiveness'. However, I think that such statements, and his leadership of the TRC and subsequent work, need to be seen in context. Tutu became an advocate for forgiving in this public sense *after* the end of apartheid and as part of a process of national reconciliation. There is a case to be made that the TRC created an environment in which insecure people might have felt pressured to 'forgive'. It was often subtle and mostly a consequence of positive reinforcement but I think it is undeniable that it was part of what happened. Nonetheless, Brudholm's focus on Tutu as the grandfather of forgiveness boosterism is unfair. No one looking at his ministry and leadership over the years could suggest that he was an uncritical proponent of political and public forgiveness in all situations.

The TRC was a response to the *end* of apartheid, not a way of coping with ongoing oppression or violence. The pragmatic political and economic needs were extremely pressing and somehow an effort needed to be made so that vengeance and hatred would not become the main sentiments determining public life. If this involved overstating the claims of forgiveness, and exaggerating the moral qualities of those who demonstrated a forgiving heart, then this is perhaps a small price to pay for the avoidance of the much-anticipated bloodbath. The more serious problem, perhaps, is that the wider world, and especially the wider *Christian* world, has brought a degree of naïvety to the way in which it has understood and interpreted the TRC so that a 'TRC myth' has been generated. It is this myth which feeds into the contemporary boosting of forgiveness. When aligned with the 'cheap grace' of therapeutic forgiveness it can put undue pressure on people to forgive where perhaps this is neither a wise nor a good thing to do.

It cannot be stressed enough that we need to be very clear in discussing these matters, whether we are talking about *ongoing* harm and violation or about events in the *past*. Among the dangers of an oversimplified 'boosted' forgiveness is that it puts pressure on people who are being oppressed, bullied or abused to tolerate the intolerable or accept the unacceptable on the grounds that they are being forgiving and therefore virtuous. There are always real dangers in creating idealized myth of forgiveness, whether it is in terms of a naïve model which does not work in reality or focusing attention on examples of heroic forgiveness. Both have the same demoralizing effect on many victims, suggesting that others find forgiveness relatively straightforward and easy.

No self-respecting Christian pastoral theology or practice of pastoral care can rest content with such a state of affairs. Our understanding of forgiveness must be as subtle and realistic as the situations themselves may be sensitive and diverse. The last thing that people need when they have encountered distressing or shattering reality is someone else's fantasy of putting things quickly and easily to rights. As John Swinton has written:

> forcing victims of evil to heed the call to forgive in a legalistic or judgemental way risks turning people into *victims of grace*, that is, people who feel oppressed, downtrodden, and dispirited because they cannot match the standard that grace sets for them. Forgiveness is a difficult and for some impossible task.[9]

## Forgiveness and Closure

Pressure to forgive can come from a variety of sources and bring and excite inappropriate expectations in terms of what is possible. One form this takes is to think that forgiveness implies or brings 'closure'. After an extraordinarily vicious home burglary in Connecticut in 2007 Dr William Petit was the only surviving member of his nuclear family. His wife Jennifer and daughters Hayley and Michaela were all tortured and killed and their home was burnt down. The two men responsible were arrested immediately afterwards and after one was tried and given the death sentence, Dr Petit was interviewed by Oprah Winfrey. She asked if there would ever be 'closure' for him. He answered:

> I don't think there's ever closure. I just... I don't think there is. People will probably argue with me, but I just don't think you can lose your whole family and have closure. Like I said, there's a jagged hole in your heart, there's a jagged hole in your soul. Over time, the waves of goodness going back and forth maybe smooth the jagged edges a little bit, but the hole remains. I don't think you'll fill it in. Forty months later, that's how I feel.[10]

Harvard Law professor Martha Minow has written against the possibility of closure after atrocity, saying even if it were possible it would 'insult those whose lives were forever ruptured'.[11] Indeed she suggests that closure is a 'temptation' to be resisted as it would be 'to avoid what remains inevitably indeterminate, elusive, and inexplicable'. [12] She is writing about what she calls 'collective horrors' but the point applies to domestic and personal ones too. Jill Scott comes to a similar conclusion at the end of her book saying that 'forgiveness must remain an unfinished practice'.[13]

The association of 'forgiveness' with 'closure' might be one reason why some forgiving people are uncomfortable with using the word. Two contributors of the book *Forgiving and Remembering in Northern Ireland,* go out of their way to articulate their reticence to speak of forgiveness. Jo Berry, whose father was killed in the Brighton bombing of 1984 has appeared in many public dialogues with the man who planted the bomb, Patrick Magee. In an interview published in the book she said:

> I know people who are doing fantastic work, who say they haven't forgiven and they don't want to, and they've got no resentment and they're fine. The idea that if you don't forgive you're somehow less of a person is not true and it's one of the reasons that I don't like to use the word. [14]

Michael Paterson was severely injured in a bomb blast in west Belfast in 1981. At the time he was a constable in the Royal Ulster Constabulary. Since then he has retrained as a clinical psychologist and has been honoured for his work with former terrorists. At the end of his moving and inspiring chapter he writes: 'The reader will note that nowhere have I said that I forgive the members of the IRA who maimed me and caused heartache, frustration and sadness, not only for me but for my family.'[15] He goes on to say that he has let go of resentment and anger and has a positive attitude instead. It is not, it seems, the reality of forgiveness that is at issue here, but the word.

Over the last two decades that word has moved from obscurity into considerable limelight. The human family has learnt a great deal during that time; it would be unfortunate if one of them was that the word 'forgiveness' is too dangerous to be used in the aftermath of shattering events. If, however, the lesson we take is that forgiveness is a slow, deep, enigmatic, unpredictable and vulnerable venture based on generosity, empathy and trust then we might be more able to cope with the unjust hurts that people still suffer from and which await many in the future.

## Forgiver Syndrome

The desire to forgive can create another problem. The issue here is not that the person feels constrained from without but that they develop the deep aspiration from within to be a forgiving person; to see themselves, and perhaps to be seen by others, as an admirable 'forgiver'. Such aspiration can easily be connected with a sense of moral superiority. To see oneself as a forgiver is potentially to see oneself as a very good person. Whereas to see oneself as someone who is still hurting too much to be able to trust again, or who is too honest about their anger and resentment to be able to smile at the person who has inflicted harm, never mind embrace them or say 'I forgive you', is to have to come to terms with something unattractive and undesirable about oneself, as well as uncomfortable.

Thus the desire to forgive can cause people to look for occasions when they can forgive. They can even begin to see situations in which they find themselves feeling uncomfortable or offended as occasions which demand from them not an answer to the question, 'how does this challenge *me*, and how might I change in the light of the new knowledge and insights that this throws up?" But, 'am I not generous and good to forgive even when the one who has so annoyed has shown no sign of repentance?' This is the 'forgiver syndrome' and all but the most vengeful and vindictive have it in some degree. Its problem is that it becomes a way of viewing the world which *assumes* that the actions of others which offend me are unjust.

If I have the syndrome I believe that when I am hurt then someone else must be at fault for hurting me. This might not be the case. I might be merely egocentric and self-defensive. It might be that my hurt is a consequence of the fact that I am the problem here, that, although I have not yet worked this out for myself, I am the guilty party, and that it is from my own actions that injustice flows. It might not be this stark. I might not be entirely to blame, but I might carry some of the responsibility, be part of the problem.

The forgiver syndrome inclines people to make a two-phase error of ethical perception. The first is to assume that occasions when they have been hurt or harmed are inevitably occasions of injustice and that their own negative feelings about it are the inner voice of justice. Feeling vindicated in resentment they move on to the second phase which is to feel virtuous in giving it up or letting it go. Moreover, the syndrome encourages people to be proactive in letting this resentment go and therefore take their self-admiration to a third level of delusion. Thus those afflicted with forgiver syndrome, and sadly this is a syndrome which escapes self-awareness, habitually claim the moral high ground. It is a sorry state and does the cause of genuine, difficult, reflective forgiveness no good at all.

To put it in a nutshell, if we seek to forgive people who have hurt us for good or at least acceptable reasons (we were perhaps being arrogant and overbearing and so someone needed to put us in our place, or we were about to hurt someone ourselves and so someone needed to stop us in our tracks) then we are not making a positive contribution to the situation at all. Rather we are persisting in the double fantasy that we are first blameless and second that we are excellent forgivers. Real forgivers, on the other hand, doubt whether they are doing it at all well and become aware, through the processes of empathy and reflection, of their own failings and shortcomings. We recall Marian Partington's 'rotting pile of mistakes', and remember our own.[16]

Luke's story of the prodigal son is seen as a powerful paradigm of Christian forgiveness. For the person with 'forgiver syndrome' or an unhealthy need to see themselves as a forgiver, the figure of the father is an attractive one. This might be blameless enough, or even positively virtuous, but it might not be. The parable is a great story of homecoming and welcome. It is also, in its uncomfortable second half where we meet the elder brother, an insightful reminder of the reality of envy and sibling rivalry. But whether it is a story of forgiveness depends on a number of assumptions that we make about it. This does not matter in the abstract but it does matter when people see the behaviour of the father as of the essence of forgiveness and therefore much to be emulated by would-be forgivers, and practised by that most expert and magnanimous of all forgivers – the self-conscious Christian.

In the previous chapter we saw one aspect of the way in which the American novelist Marilynne Robinson draws on the parable of the prodigal son in her novel *Gilead*. As a sequel to that she wrote the parallel novel, *Home*. Whereas *Gilead* is narrated by the elderly Reverend John Ames, *Home* is written in the third person, often reflecting the perspective of 38-year-old Glory Boughton who has returned home to care for her father and life-long friend of Ames, the Reverend Robert Boughton. Glory's wayward brother Jack returns home after twenty years and there is a happy meal, like the old days. But as this is a novel rather than a parable there is plenty of time and space to explore the complexity of the situation that arises.

One factor in this is that both Jack's father (Boughton) and his godfather (Ames) see themselves as struggling with forgiveness. We have already seen that in Ames' view the parable of the prodigal son is intended to put the reader in the position of the father. Boughton does precisely this, and therein lies part of the tragedy. His struggle is focused on the restoration and maintenance of his household. His desire is to welcome Jack back, but on his own terms. The reader soon realizes that for Jack, this was a suffocating and unhelpful environment in which to grow up. This begins to explain, but not to excuse, some of Jack's youthful misdemeanours and even acts of cruelty. We know that Jack's upbringing has been somewhat lacking; had his father been more accommodating and open to his needs, he might have grown up differently and become more comfortable with himself, an easier member of the household and less of a reprobate. But there is more to Jack than being either a black sheep or a lost sheep. Jack is not only a victim of an oppressive household, he is also a kind of prophetic figure, offering both theological and ethical challenge to both men and drawing attention to complacency regarding racial injustice into which the town has fallen under their spiritual leadership.

In the first of the two novels, *Gilead*, we learn of John Ames' reflections over the period of Jack's return and some conversations with him. During the course of this we see a change in his attitude. While he begins with the reading of the prodigal son which challenges him to be like the father in the story and forgive, that desire modulates as over time he reflects on it until in the end it becomes the desire to *bless*. It is a profound, positive and healthy development. It is a gesture that speaks of divine love and human acceptance and yet does not imply that Jack's behaviour is condoned. It certainly suggests a very different relationship than one framed by the story of the prodigal son, and that, I suggest, is Ames' spiritual breakthrough. The story of the prodigal son has a great deal to teach us about the theology of forgiving and about family dynamics, but it does not model a 'one size fits all' forgiveness paradigm.

For instance, Jesus' story in Luke's gospel does not tell us what the son brought home. It tells us of his change of heart, his 'coming to himself' when among the pig troughs. It does *not* tell us whether, once the fatted calf has been eaten, he is treated as a respected adult member of the community who has a voice that is heard. That might be an overly modern expectation to bring to the text, but anyone who seeks to do justice to the desire to forgive today must, I suggest, be aware of the importance of such issues. The danger of the 'forgiver syndrome' is that it overly defines people in terms of being *either* the forgiver *or* the forgiven; *either* the prodigal son *or* the forgiving father.

Some situations are like this but many are not and simply to transport this paradigm into such situations is to distort forgiveness in such a way as to make people feel virtuous or even god-like when the truth is that they need to be on the receiving end as much as on the giving end of forgiveness. A mature and healthy reading of the parable of the prodigal son requires that we identify with all three characters, even the most unattractive one – the elder brother. Like Henri Nouwen, the serious forgiver will also be serious about their own need to repent and say 'the more I think about the elder son, the more I recognize myself in him'.[17] True, deep and costly forgiveness begins not when we think we should be more like the father (or God) but when we realize that we are like both the younger and the elder brother.

## Reflection

It is not easy to interpret, apply or live the message of forgiveness which is integral to following Jesus and living the life of the new covenant revealed in the New Testament. In this chapter we have identified two excesses of the desire to forgive. They are 'forgiveness boosterism' which manipulates people into a false forgiveness, and 'forgiver syndrome' which afflicts those who so want to be able to forgive that they fail to understand their own need to change and seek forgiveness. Our study of the *Duty to Forgive* and of *Forgiveness as Spirituality*, as well as what we have learnt from reading some deep forgiveness stories, suggests that if we are to develop a positive understanding of forgiveness we will need to avoid anything which encourages naïve and simplistic models of forgiveness or which exacerbates the tendency of some to indulge in disempowering 'forgiveness boosterism' or in the self-flattering 'forgiver syndrome'.

We have also reflected on the very natural and common desire for forgiveness to bring an end to suffering after hurt. People who have been through shattering events often long for a way of transcending them and bringing their traumatic re-living and troubled recriminations to an end, and so too do their companions. This is the desire for 'closure'. This deep longing may never be extinguished, the line under the past may never be drawn. This is perhaps most obviously the case when a loved one has been maimed or where a person carries constant pain or severe disability in the aftermath of hurt.

But in the aftermath of hurt much suffering is internal and goes unseen. Forgiving might help people live with the consequences of harm and hurt but will not eliminate the consequences. As many have observed, in some cases forgiving is something which has to begin afresh everyday. In this way it is like both grief and love. The jagged hole within is something which the wise forgiver will seek not to close, but to live with.

Forgiveness is slow, deep, enigmatic, unpredictable and vulnerable. This conclusion, if absorbed, might be an antidote to the forgiver syndrome and help us resist the temptation to believe that closure might be achieved in order that the hurt of hurt may be entirely eliminated. It is certainly a conclusion that means that we will move forward from events which have seriously hurt us with care and gentleness, as well as resolve.

Should we find ourselves in the company of those who have been damaged, distressed or shattered by the unjust actions of others, we will be of far more help and support to them if we recognize and honour these truths and are both positive about human forgiveness and realistic about its limits.

## Notes

1. Lamb, S. and Murphy, J. G . (eds) *Before Forgiving*, p. ix.
2. Garrard, E. and McNaughton, D. *Forgiveness*, p. 29.
3. Brudholm, T. *Resentment's Virtue*, p. 51.
4. Brudholm, T. *Resentment's Virtue*, p. 52 (original emphasis).
5. Brudholm, T. *Resentment's Virtue*, p. 53.
6. I have written about this at length in Watts, F. and Gulliford, L. *Forgiveness in Context.*
7. See Lapsley's story at: http://theforgivenessproject.org.uk.
8. One of the reasons for looking at forgiveness stories is that they are often different in both obvious and subtle ways. They also change over time. Lapsley could be interpreted in a number of ways here but it is important not to compare his attitude with that of someone who has met the person who harmed them or who knows that the person is now serving a jail sentence. His story is important because few are able to articulate the need for practical restitution as part of a just future. I read this as a forgiveness story that has stalled and which requires some input from the perpetrator to be able to move forward. In this way it encapsulates many of the South African issues which were not adequately addressed by the TRC or legal processes at the time of transition. That is the underlying issues of justice and economics. The cost of harm and hurt are not driven away by a forgiving spirit. The future which forgiveness allows is one with practical demands and sometimes the one who has caused harm will need to know how to live with and share the consequences. Human forgiveness does not by itself transform the consequences of hurtful acts.
9. Swinton, J. *Raging with Compassion*, p. 167.
10. http://www.oprah.com/showinfo/Dr-William-Petit-on-the-Unspeakable-Tragedy-in-Connecticut, 9 December 2010.
11. Minow, M. *Between Vengeance and Forgiveness*, p. 5.
12. Minow, M. *Between Vengeance and Forgiveness*, p. 24.

13. Scott, J. *A Poetics of Forgiveness*, p. 200.
14. Spencer, G. *Forgiving and Remembering in Northern Ireland*, p. 226.
15. Spencer, G. *Forgiving and Remembering in Northern Ireland*, p. 197.
16. See above, p. 109.
17. Nouwen, H. M. *The Return of the Prodigal Son*, p. 69.

## CHAPTER 9

# Visiting Evil

One of the most compelling and insightful books to come out of the Truth and Reconciliation (TRC) process in South Africa is by one of the commissioners who was also a clinical psychologist. Pumla Gobodo-Madikizela tells the story of her visits to the maximum security prison to meet with Eugene de Kock who was serving a two hundred and twelve-year sentence for the crimes committed under the apartheid regime. The book is subtitled 'A South African Story of Forgiveness' but it might more accurately be called a story of the complexity and pain of empathy. De Kock had become known as 'Prime Evil' and, as Gobodo-Madikizela remarks, had come to represent all that was bad about the apartheid regime. As she reflects on her first visit she writes: 'The embodiment of evil stood there politely smiling at me.'[1].

Gobodo-Madikizela began to visit de Kock after he first appeared at a TRC hearing. He had testified to his role in killing three black policemen. Afterwards he met the widows who subsequently met with Gobodo-Madikizela who was assigned to debrief them on the experience. She was amazed by what she heard. They spoke of being 'profoundly touched by him'. He acknowledged their pain. There were tears, and one of them, Mrs Pearl Faku, said:

I was overwhelmed by emotion, and I was just nodding, as a

> way of saying, yes, I forgive you. I hope that when he sees our tears, he knows that they are not only tears for our husbands, but tears for him as well… I would like to hold him by the hand, and show him that there is a future, and that he can still change.[2]

Listening to the women talk about their attitude towards de Kock caused Gobodo-Madikizela to reflect deeply on the nature of forgiveness. Was this a step too far? Was de Kock, as Prime Evil, worthy of this? But more profoundly, 'Was evil intrinsic to de Kock, and forgiveness therefore wasted on him?'[3] Such questions were on her mind as she embarked on a long series of visits which would inevitably involve the possibility of coming to know and understand this 'Prime Evil'.[4] She was nervous about it, wondering about the ethics and propriety of even seeking to understand such a perpetrator. Her fear was that if she even began to understand she might be drawn into excusing, and that would be outrageous and obscene.[5] Nonetheless the book tells the story of a growing relationship.

Gobodo-Madikizela shares with the reader her anguish as she gets to know more of the man. She reflects on the horrifying details of his activities but also hears him tell stories which reveal his struggles with guilt and feels herself some of the relief that testifying before the TRC was able to bring to him. But despite her own background growing up in the violence of apartheid South Africa and working to support the victims who appeared before the TRC and developing 'powerfully empathic relations with them', she also experienced empathy for de Kock. But she was not at all comfortable with it:

> To experience empathy for someone who has committed

> terrible acts against other human beings, as I did with Eugene de Kock, puts one in a strangely compelling and confusing relationship with the perpetrator.[6]

One of the focal moments in this relationship takes place when he becomes distressed when talking about his meeting with the two widows:

> Relating to him the only way one does in such human circumstances, I touched his shaking hand, surprising myself. But it was clenched, cold, and rigid, as if he were holding back, as if he were holding on to some withering but still vital form of his old self. This made me recoil for a moment and to recast my spontaneous act of reaching out as something incompatible with the circumstances of an encounter with a person who not too long ago had used these same hands, this same voice, to authorize and initiate unspeakable acts of malice against people very much like myself.[7]

The following morning, however, she found that she could not lift her right forearm. It had become temporarily paralyzed. As a psychologist, Gobodo-Madikizela understood this as a manifestation of 'splitting'. She was splitting off the part of the self that had been in touch with evil. The next time they met he referred back to the moment of touch. It was an unscheduled meeting in a tearoom during a break at a TRC hearing. 'Then, with an expression that seemed to reflect genuine amazement, he said: "You know Pumla, that was my trigger hand you touched."'[8]

It is a scene that focuses a great deal of the tension, anguish and agony that is implicit in any form of forgiveness in the aftermath of violation or atrocity. The 'forgiver' reaches out to they know not what. They move into a real danger zone.

They take a step into a place where they could be physically vulnerable, spiritually uncomfortable and ethically very unsure of themselves. To move into such territory clearly had a major and confusing impact on Gobodo-Madikizela:

> I have not, up until now, been able to free myself from the grip of that statement nor to soften its visceral impact. It was a remark pregnant with so many confusing and contradictory messages. It seemed to unveil the dark pleasures of a man who, at one point, not only had enjoyed inflicting considerable pain on others but also had perhaps relished imagining and reimagining how they must have felt, and had drawn strength and pride from watching others express revulsion when he regaled them with graphic stories from the field.
>
> De Kock certainly had succeeded in making short shrift of any sort of boundary between interviewer and subject. He had penetrated my defenses. I felt invaded, naked, angry.[9]

Referring back to the incident of the frozen forearm, she realized that she was also being drawn into de Kock's world of personal fragmentation. His notion of the trigger hand was a way of distancing himself from his actions in an act of self-preservation. 'But it was also an illustration of how fragmented he was – a person broken into bits struggling to achieve some sense of wholeness.'[10] Yet he was not alone in this condition for she goes on to write:

> I was aware of disintegration happening within myself. I was struggling with the part of me that made it possible to identify with de Kock – the evil de Kock. In a way, it was through 'splitting' that I was able to do this, for in my mind

> I had managed to separate the evil deeds from the doer, and could embrace the side of de Kock that showed some of the positive elements of being human.[11]

Gobodo-Madikizela underlines here a central aspect of forgiveness: the costliness and danger that are involved for the forgiver. This is in part because the empathy required of the forgiver draws them into the chaotic, broken and possibly cruel world of the perpetrator. This is to venture into the most uninviting and unattractive territory. It is a different and yet parallel venture to that of going into the wilderness of hurt. Different in that the victim has no choice (precisely as victim) as to whether they enter that wilderness. They are thrust into it by events beyond their control.

On the other hand, a degree of personal freedom is needed to be able to make the decision to enter by empathy into the world and mind of the perpetrator. Such a journey is not undertaken with a view to explaining away or excusing the harmful or violating behaviour. In fact, it is less difficult and painful to excuse someone as that does not involve seeking to understand at this empathic level. Nor does it mean that to understand all is to forgive all, as if forgiveness is an inevitable corollary of empathy.

Empathy is a matter of degree and indeed gravity, but, in cases where the empathy is with a perpetrator of unjust and harmful acts, the empathizer has in some way to engage with and respond to the reality of the mind and heart that was the cause of their hurt. Forgiveness is not just a matter of empathy but it is only when empathy develops that we move into the place where forgiveness might be possible. For forgiveness comes not from objectivity and distance but subjectivity and relationship. Forgiveness requires genuine intimacy. Just to say this is to underline the horror and anguish of it for victims of violation and betrayal.

In a further intensification of the relationship, de Kock did one day ask her whether he had ever killed any of her friends or family. The question revealed his anguish and increased hers:

> I looked at de Kock, searching deep within in his eyes, reading between the lines for signs of evil, of malice. His eyes were filled with suffering, I felt nothing but pity, the kind one feels when a friend is in pain over an event that has deeply troubled him. I stared at his face again, and for a moment I thought I might touch him – *again?* – to offer him some respite from the tortured emotions that seemed to be coursing through his brain and body. But how? Where could I touch him? The awkwardness of reaching out to someone, almost six feet tall, who had killed many of my people, and to do it in front of the black guards... What would *they* think? What would de Kock think? This black woman reaching out to him with an embrace?[12]

Gobodo-Madikizela tells the reader that even if he had killed her loved ones she would never be able to tell him and she says: 'No Eugene. No one close to me.' It was what she heard when he asked the question that formed the response. 'Ultimately, what I heard was the voice of an outcast begging to rejoin the world of the living. His past, it seems, was unbearable. But his future, stained as it was with the memory of lives snuffed out, was also unbearable.'[13]

Gobodo-Madikizela does not tell us how truthful or disingenuous her reply was, and in a way it does not matter for she has already given many clues to the extent to which she identified with his victims: she calls them, 'my people'. It would be wrong, however, to see in such statements a mere reversal of what she calls the apartheid of the mind: an internalization of the split between bad them and good us. It is rather a reflection of that way of thinking about personhood and identity which is summarized in the concept of *ubuntu*.

The idea is not unique to African sensibility but this word has been used to draw attention to its importance in forming the kind of solidarity which was integral both to the end of apartheid and to the reconciliatory dynamic of the post apartheid era. The core idea is that human beings are not fundamentally different and distinct, not free floating individuals who happen to make relationships, but that relationship and connectedness are fundamental to being human.

Phrases such as 'I am because we are' summarize the idea, though there is no word in English that quite captures the meaning of the one word *ubuntu*. Such an *ubuntu* mentality does, however, provide a different context for forgiveness than does a more individualistic culture. For it is a certain kind of individualism which suggests that it is the victim only who can forgive. The kind of empathy which Gobodo-Madikizela is describing is a reflection of an *ubuntu* approach to life in the aftermath of serious unjust harm in which commonalty and community are more important than the distinctive qualities or experiences of individuals. In this way, Gobodo-Madikizela's thinking is in line with that of Desmond Tutu, whose theology reflects the primacy of relationship and community while at the same time emphasizing the importance of personal responsibility, not least in exercising generosity and creativity in the aftermath of violation.

The pain of empathy was integral to her involvement in the TRC. She tells us how profoundly she empathized with other victims of torture and abuse. Reporting how she felt when Yvonne Khutwane told of how a young soldier, the age of her own children, had pushed his hand into her vagina in the back of a police truck when she has been arrested, she writes,

> Then I pictured her in the back of the army truck, her body being violated by a white soldier in camouflage uniform, and I feel every detail of her trauma as if it is something that has happened to me: the intrusive hand of the young soldier, the shame of helplessness, and the humiliation all seem like a painful stab deep inside… The feeling was so intense that I choked with tears. A fellow committee member next to me on the stage reached out to stroke my back to comfort me. The gesture brought me back to my senses so to speak. I had to regain my composure.[14]

Yet she also records that the empathy was not only agony. It was also healing.

> At the end of the Worcester hearings, Mrs Khutwane had looked for me to tell me how healing she had found my show of emotion during her testimony. 'I felt you were connecting with my pain at a deep level, and that someone understood what I went through,' she explained.[15]

Knowing that another person has connected with my pain at a deep level, that they have in a way felt it, is one of the ways in which human beings are healed and reconciled into community. Being empathized with, and indeed empathizing with others, is also part of the process that forms our moral character and spiritual personality. People doubtless vary in the readiness with which they experience empathy. Some are very resistant and defensive regarding the pain of others. Others are more easily moved. Some respond to a real person in real time, others only allow the experience of the others in if they read about it in private.

When we do so we speak of being 'moved' by what we read. We usually do this with a degree of gratitude, recognizing that it matters that we are thus moved. Indeed it does. It offers no healing to the person whose words we read, but it does exercise and strengthen that capacity we have which, if engaged in real life, can bring healing and hope and lead to forgiveness.[16]

Empathy is integral to *ubuntu*. But while that is true of empathy with the victim, forgiveness also involves empathy for the perpetrator on the part of the victim and that is why forgiveness is a kind of agony. This is one of the reasons why ruthless vengeance can be a more attractive prospect. But it is also a reason why simple tolerance can be attractive too. Either seems to offer an end to agony. It is a matter of judgement as to which is the better or more lasting. Those who advocate vengeance might argue that it is only when you have vanquished your foe that you can properly relax and that the tolerant are doomed to oppression and suffering. Those who are in favour of forgiveness would bring other considerations to bear. They might, for instance. believe that the vanquished foe is never truly vanquished and that after the reprisal they will simply be awaiting an opportunity to turn the tables. This is the view which believes that vengeance begets vengeance: the spiral of violence.

One of the points at issue between those who would follow a path of vengeance and those who would advocate and seek to practise forgiveness concerns which is the weaker response, or which has the more positive consequences. Gobodo-Madikizela comments that, 'although forgiveness is often regarded as an expression of weakness, the decision to forgive can paradoxically elevate a victim to a position of strength as the one who holds the key to the perpetrator's wish.'[17] She recognizes that if forgiveness is merely understood as granting the perpetrator's wishes then it might 'appear to condone' the offence and disempower the victim. But true forgiveness does not work like this, 'forgiveness does not overlook the deed: it rises above it. "This is what it means to be human," it says. "I cannot and will not return the evil you inflicted on me." And that is the victim's triumph.' She sees this as a kind of revenge, 'but revenge enacted at a rarefied level'. Forgiveness is humanizing for the victim, the perpetrator and the bystander.

Gobodo-Madikizela emphasizes that there is a 'feel-good' factor in forgiving.

> There was nothing as satisfying as returning from an interview with de Kock and realizing that I could not regard him with the same dehumanizing hatred and disdain that he had trained on his victims. In fact, I did not want hatred to make *me* his victim.[18]

She is clear about this: the power of forgiveness is its capacity to end generational cycles of violence. The triumph of the forgiver is not to vanquish the foe but to change the rules of engagement. This is exactly what was attempted not only by the TRC but by the decision to make 'reconciliation' one of the pillars of the constitution of the new South Africa. Forgiveness is unattractive and difficult for those who experience anger or resentment and who, in the absence of acknowledgement, regret or remorse, see such feelings as a way of maintaining the truth that wrong was done, injustice perpetrated. Gobodo-Madikizela argues that, 'not to forgive means closing the door to the possibility of transformation'.[19] The danger in arguing this is that it makes forgiveness an operational tactic in a wider process.

Jacques Derrida believes that this is what happened in South Africa and that it is essentially a degrading of pure forgiveness. His objection is ideological; he is worried about forgiveness being 'taken too lightly'. 'Forgiveness does not, it should never amount to a therapy of reconciliation.'[20] There are genuinely difficult issues here. If forgiveness is transformative of cycles of violence and vengeance then it has real political potency. However, if that power is corrupted as soon as people try to 'use' forgiveness in a political or public process then maybe that transformative power is either lost or in danger of being corrupted or annexed to unworthy ends.

Thomas Brudholm criticized those involved in the TRC process for failing to recognize that forgiveness and vengeance were not merely alternatives but poles of a possible spectrum of responses:

> This stark dichotomy of either forgiveness or vengeance–hatred–bitterness does not do justice to the actual spectrum of possible attitudinal responses between those two emotional poles. The rhetorical evocation of vengeance as forgiveness' demonic other does not appropriately capture the position of victims who seek just legal prosecution and punishment of the wrongdoers.[21]

Brudholm also suggests that in the TRC there was a tendency to pathologize those who did not take the path of forgiveness. Anger and resentment were seen as embittering and debilitating and the commissioners and others encouraged victims to forgive so that they might derive the health benefits that come to forgivers (this is the 'forgiveness is good for you' argument of those who espouse therapeutic forgiveness). He is right to suggest that maybe some questionable assumptions were made and helpfully cites Lawrence Langer's essay comparing issues of justice and memory after the holocaust and apartheid. He writes:

> Holocaust survivors may continue to despise those who betrayed, brutalized or murdered their kind, but anyone who hears their testimony (or knows them personally) will instantly recognize that such feelings, while (understandably) affecting their outlook, have not succeeded in poisoning their lives.[22]

The point comes from a different context but does have relevance. It is possible to retain focused indignation in such a way as not to ruin your own life or health, and sometimes justice might require this of us. Moreover, there are times when it might be appropriate to sacrifice our own well-being to the cause of justice. Personal well-being is not the ultimate ethical criterion. There are risks in holding on to indignation or resentment, just as there are risks in being more overtly forgiving. The path taken will depend on both subjective and objective factors. While it might be right for one person to encourage another to explore forgiving in one situation, this has few implications for the way in which someone else will advise a different person in another situation.

What happened in the TRC happened in a particular transitional context and should neither be judged by the criteria relevant in other situations nor seen as prescribing what should or could happen elsewhere. It was apparently the judgement of the commissioners that the political transition meant that forgiveness, which would have been inappropriate had apartheid oppression continued, was now virtuous and so to be encouraged. Previously impossible and out of place, such generosity of spirit articulated as forgiveness was seen as both miraculous and appropriate.

What critics of 'forgiveness boosterism' require us to recognize is that taking an understanding of forgiveness formed by Christian doctrine and contemporary psychological understanding into the public and political domain at a time of historical upheaval was a very risky venture. Mistakes and oversimplifications were inevitable. This suggests not that forgiveness is never appropriate but that we would be unwise to take TRC as a model for any other process or allow expression of forgiveness from that context to set a benchmark for forgiving.

None of this, however, detracts from the forgiveness that the TRC did facilitate or from the truth that the word 'forgiveness' does have psychological and ethical meaning and that from time to time people find themselves to be willing participants in a forgiveness story. Such stories are possibly rarer than champions of forgiveness would like to believe. Equally, they are often much less well structured than we might imagine and are rarely driven by a strong character seeking heroically to forgive.

Finally, we might observe that the story that Gobodo-Madikizela tells us is an informative one partly because, while it has its origins in a TRC process, it is not contaminated by questions of amnesty. The forgiven man remains in jail serving his two hundred and twelve-year sentence. Had he been given amnesty it would be a different story, possibly not a 'forgiveness story'.

Every act of forgiveness takes place in a wider historical, social and political context and to varying degrees each act of forgiveness has an impact on that wider context. To see forgiveness as a process or action that an isolated resentful individual may undertake under certain conditions – where, for instance, the objective demands of justice are adequately met – is to fail to see the inevitable embeddedness of that act of harm and its consequences, as well as any subsequent process which emerges, be that vengeful or forgiving. Real forgiveness always takes place in a messy context: a spiritual, ethical, relational eco-system, but it is never fully determined by its context and has the capacity to have a transformative effect on the surrounding ecology.

Whether that transformative potential can ever be captured by a commission or a psychological process we cannot be sure. But there is an important and multilayered conversation being conducted between what we might call 'forgiveness' and the public political realm in which it will always be difficult to identify cause and effect. Keeping that conversation going, learning from the dialogue, the triumphs and the mistakes, does seem to be a responsible activity. It is not as helpful as it may at first appear to see vengeance and forgiveness as alternatives, nor to hope that healing space can be opened up between the extremes. The question of forgiveness, rather, is a matter of incorporating *and* transcending both emotional and ethical considerations and working on through the contingencies of character and circumstance until the victim is victim no more.

Jill Scott sees forgiveness as a continuum, 'ranging from the first doubt about justified revenge to neutral acceptance to exuberant love for the wrongdoer'.[23] In her view the practice of forgiveness includes endless small gestures and intentions. But more than this, she writes that she 'would go so far as to include resentment and vindictive emotions within the spectrum of forgiving because they are often present through the forgiving process and may even arise years later'.[24]

Gobodo-Madikizela argues that the pressing question is

whether our social ecology encourages or inhibits forgiveness. She writes that, 'the question is no longer whether victims can forgive evildoers but whether we – our symbols, language and politics, our legal, media and academic institutions – are creating the conditions that can generate alternatives to revenge'.[25] This is a question not only for nations emerging from years of tyranny or oppression but for both domestic and national life at any point in time. The question is whether we dare to hope for a culture in which those who offend, injure or violate others are regarded as so different that they need to be punished or isolated (or both) or whether they need to be regarded as fellows by us (and by 'us' I mean the direct victims, the indirect victims and the wider community of bystanders and side-takers).

Put at its most simple, the question is this: when we are talking of those who have unjustly, and sometimes very severely, hurt, injured or violated others, are we talking about 'them' or are we talking about 'us'. It is a simple question, but the psychology, ethics, spirituality and politics of it are complex and difficult, both when we are the victim and when we are a closely connected third party.

## Distasteful Empathy

One of the reasons why I have given such extended attention to Gobodo-Madikizela's account is that I believe that the central issue she raised is fundamental to the psychology, and therefore the reality, of forgiveness. It is the question of distasteful empathy:

> One reason we distance ourselves through anger from those who have hurt us or others we know is the fear that if we engage them as real people, we will be compromising our

> moral stance and lowering the entry requirements into the human community. Part of my own struggle in my visits with de Kock stemmed from my fear of stepping into the shoes of a murderer through empathy.[26]

One of the most profound problems facing the forgiving attitude is that of imagination. We cannot imagine what it might be like to forgive those who have most seriously harmed us. That is part of our experience in the 'wilderness of hurt'. There are various reasons for this, including the normal psychological responses to abnormal experience and the focusing of our mind and attention on our physical and psychological pain during and after trauma. But the problem of distasteful empathy is an important part of this for the community of those who in some degree empathize with the victim.

When we hear the stories of victims it is relatively easy to identify with them. Most of us are hard-wired to respond – as we are to a baby's cries of distress. But what does it mean to begin to empathize with a person who has, for instance, committed a violent crime against an older person? What does it mean to empathize with a serial killer, whether one who is in a sense doing his job like de Kock or any of the Nazi leaders or guards in a Nazi concentration camp or someone like Peter Sutcliffe or Rosemary West? What does it mean to extend empathy to a paedophile or rapist?

The words themselves cause us to recoil with horror – and rightly so. To empathize with the cruel is to take your imagination to a very dangerous place, the place where cruelty becomes possible. That seems to be at the heart of the matter. In order to empathize with the cruel and heartless you have to imagine being cruel and heartless yourself. But the logic is running on too quickly here. To imagine being cruel and heartless is precisely *not* to be heartless. It is to be quite the opposite. It is to take on a heart-rending, heart-breaking task because, unlike the cruel, those who would empathize with them in a forgiveness process also empathize with the victim of the cruelty. And that's the agony.

To empathize exclusively with the cruel and heartless *is* to risk becoming heartless. But to empathize with the cruel and heartless *while at the same time* empathizing with their victims is to risk being heart-broken and that, alas, is the step the forgiver has to take. It is the risk of emotional crucifixion. This, at least, is how it seems from the perspective of the bystander. But the perspective of the victim can be put in a similar way.

The victim who empathizes with the perpetrator risks losing touch with their own hurt and their anger or resentment at its injustice. That this happens is without doubt. It is precisely the engine of the sort of tolerance that indulges the tyrant, bully or abuser. The victim, in order to be a forgiving victim, needs to remain in touch with her or his own unjust hurt, his or her victimhood, while reaching out empathically to the perpetrator. The wise victim knows that forgiveness begins in the wilderness of hurt and cannot happen unless they acknowledge that that is where they find themselves.

Gobodo-Madikizela writes: 'Empathy reaches out to the other and says: I can feel the pain you feel for having caused me pain.'[27] But that is only half of the matter. For what they really need to say is this, 'although my heart if full of the pain that you caused me, I am seeking to find some space for the pain that you yourself feel for having caused me that pain'. Put this way, it is clear that forgiveness takes serious time, cannot be guaranteed, might never be concluded and certainly cannot be forced. Yet it also begins to become apparent that forgiveness is something which is not an option but a duty for those who believe that true fulfilment can only be found where there is, under God, a degree of solidarity or fellowship between human beings that can, without irony, be called 'community' or 'communion'.

I do not believe that it is possible to make this easy. A prison chaplain once told me something of how he felt when, in the course of his duties, he put the bread of Holy Communion into the hands of a prisoner who had raped, murdered and then eaten his victim. Holy Communion has many levels and dimensions of meaning but one of them is forgiveness and an other is connectedness. We are invited by the sacrament to see the commonality, the fellowship and solidarity, of *all* who participate. In such a case as this, its challenge is to see, in the face of the horrifying other, something of your self and to see in their hands the evidence that God's forgiveness goes ahead of the human capacity.

As Gobodo-Madikizela began to grow comfortable using de Kock's first name she shared with her colleagues her growing empathy with him. She was curious about their responses. They were inclined to see it as romantic, mysterious or even kinky. But she rejected these as ways to deny or dismiss the significance of a serious attempt, 'to understand the inner mind of evil, to follow its thought processes, and to expose myself to its human face, stripped of media stereotypes and the easy distance of hatred'.[28] She adds:

> Connecting on a human level with a monster therefore comes to be a profoundly frightening prospect, for ultimately, it forces us to confront the potential for evil within ourselves. Compassion toward and hence forgiveness of people who have left a gruesome trail in their wake in effect brings 'innocent' victims and wicked men together to share at a simple common table of humanity, and the prospect is unpalatable.[29]

And rightly so; it is good to be revolted and disgusted by acts which hurt others, especially by those so devastating that they profoundly violate the other, not only humiliating them but shattering their sense of who they are. The effects of the cruel abuse of power are terrible and the instinct to rage and scream against it is one of the ways in which human beings hold their societies together and maintain solidarity with victims. When wanton cruelty passes without comment or feeling then we are as far from community and communion as it is possible to be; which is an indirect way of saying that we are in hell.

But there is only one way out of the hell into which we can be inflicted by others, the hell of the disintegrating self and the collapse of hope (that is, any prospect of a healed future) and that is through the healing of the brokenness and pain which lies at the heart of the victim. To be in receipt of empathic listening, maybe for many years, is part of the healing. Through it, the broken heart begins to be made whole again. The sense of being understood and accepted allows the knitting together of the alienated aspects of the inner self and the bearing of unbearable memories and, in situations where bereavement has been inflicted, unbearable loss, running into the future. This is itself an amazing testimony to human healing and listening, and yet all this is but the first phase in a process that might go on to include forgiveness.

For the next phase to begin, the victim will need to accept the rightness of their rage and resentment and get to a place where the humanity of the person who perpetrated violating injustice against them comes into the equation as vulnerable and perhaps broken. The forgiving victim begins to see that the perpetrator's humanity is at stake and, surprisingly, this begins to matter to them. The forgiving victim, or, perhaps better, the victim with a forgiving heart, takes an empathic interest in the person of the perpetrator. This empathic interest might begin when there is some intimation of remorse or regret. The victim will then want to know whether or not it can be trusted.

On the other hand, it might begin when the victim reaches out in disinterested generosity to the perpetrator, intuiting perhaps that no happy, unburdened person could ever do such a thing and that the hurtful actions themselves point to some prior story which shows that the perpetrator was a victim. Yet, perceiving this, the wise forgiving victim will not rush for the easy response of excusing: saying that the perpetrator was once so hurt that we should now expect them to hurt others, that their past both adequately explains their action and exonerates them.

The wise victim will avoid this line of argument because they can see in it no end to the endless cycle of abuse leading to abuse, violence to violence, vengeance to vengeance. Rather they will say, 'that was not right. There is no excuse; while I am still suffering the consequences I do not need to hold on to any aspect of those consequences in order to assert my own dignity or the outrage of what happened. Let me then see if I can let go of anger, resentment and grudge. Let me unlock the cold punishment cell within my own inner being where I keep the perpetrator incarcerated and let me welcome them, as best I can, into my own empathic imagination so that maybe there might be some healing for them too. I do this not only because it will be good for me to have that inner prison cell vacated since resentment, anger and grudge are all burdens to carry, but also because this is the main contribution that I can make to breaking the cycle of vengeance which is so much more destructive than any particular harmful act, however evil and hurtful.'

Or, to put it in terms of Christian theology: 'I will offer forgiveness because this is the one thing within my gift as victim which is a contribution to the coming of the kingdom of God.' Put like this, we can begin to see forgiveness as the *gift of myself as victim*.

The result is a kind of resurrection. Victim no more, the one who has suffered unjustly not only survives but triumphs. This triumph is not, however, a triumph over the former persecutor or violator in which one wins and the other looses. True forgiveness is not zero-sum reversal of the apparently irreversible. It is a matter of transcendence, a true resurrection. It is not the perpetrator who is defeated. Indeed the perpetrator is offered the opportunity for healing and freedom. It is the heavy, dead and deadening power of evil that is thwarted by forgiveness. The victory is of grace over evil, of empathy over cruelty. The triumph is of healing generosity over alienating meanness. The forgiving heart chooses life and in return for its yielded victim status receives newness and abundance of life. One of the characteristics of this is an increased capacity to forgive and so the virtuous circle goes on, causing and facilitating further change in the wider eco-system of sin and its consequences.

It must be stressed that this process of forgiving is not conducted at the expense of justice. Just because Pumla Gobodo-Madikizela touched de Kock's trigger hand and called him by his first name does not mean that the state should give him amnesty. Just because a murderer receives Holy Communion does not mean that they should be released from prison. Whether or not long-term imprisonment serves the aims of justice is a moot point but not one that we need to discuss here.

The issue that needs to be clarified and reinforced is that justice processes and forgiveness processes concern different matters. Justice processes concern the relationship between the state or community and the person who has broken laws.

Forgiveness processes, however, take place at the level of relationships. The norm of a forgiveness process is between the victim and the perpetrator but, as I have argued earlier, that is too narrow a compass within which to describe the workings of a forgiving spirit. Our wide-angle concern is with the ways in which human beings make progress through the stony territory of the wilderness of hurt, without either denying the problem and condoning the offender or responding in such a way that reinforces the dynamic of harmful injustice which propelled them into that desert in first place.

This close reading of Pumla Gobodo-Madikizela's *A Human Being Died That Night* has shown us how a distasteful empathy is integral to this process and that, ultimately, forgiveness is achieved when the victim not only resists the temptation to hate and sheds their legitimate feelings of resentment but actually makes a gift of themselves as victim.

The gift is healing. The journey that makes it possible can be agony.

## Notes

1. Gobodo-Madikizela, P. *A Human Being Died That Night*, p. 6.
2. Gobodo-Madikizela, P. *A Human Being Died That Night*, pp. 14–15.
3. Gobodo-Madikizela, P. *A Human Being Died That Night*, p. 15.
4. She visited him over a period of six months for forty-six hours in total, p. 17.
5. Gobodo-Madikizela, P. *A Human Being Died That Night* p. 17.
6. Gobodo-Madikizela, P. *A Human Being Died That Night* p. 79.
7. Gobodo-Madikizela, P. *A Human Being Died That Night*, p. 32.
8. Gobodo-Madikizela, P. *A Human Being Died That Night*, p. 39.
9. Gobodo-Madikizela, P. *A Human Being Died That Night*, pp. 39–40.
10. Gobodo-Madikizela, P. *A Human Being Died That Night*, p. 41.
11. Gobodo-Madikizela, P. *A Human Being Died That Night*, pp. 41–42.
12. Gobodo-Madikizela, P. *A Human Being Died That Night*, pp. 114–15.

13. Gobodo-Madikizela, P. *A Human Being Died That Night*, p. 115.
14. Gobodo-Madikizela, P. *A Human Being Died That Night*, p. 91–2.
15. Gobodo-Madikizela, P. *A Human Being Died That Night*, p. 93.
16. When discussing photography and forgiveness, Jill Scott develops Susan Sontag's concern about the capacity of war photographs to have a numbing effect. The distinction that she draws is between feeling empathy and being overwhelmed by the way in which another's pain evokes fear in us. 'Rather than empathizing with the victims of violence, we identify with their pain and become crippled by the fear that we too might suffer such a fate,' Scott, J. *A Poetics of Forgiveness*, p133. This distinction is relevant to the question of how a victim might be enabled to come to embrace what Scott calls the 'precariousness' of forgiveness.
17. All quotes in this paragraph, Gobodo-Madikizela, P. *A Human Being Died That Night*, p. 17.
18. Gobodo-Madikizela, P. *A Human Being Died That Night*, p. 118.
19. Gobodo-Madikizela, P. *A Human Being Died That Night*, p. 103.
20. Derrida, J. *On Cosmopolitanism and Forgiveness*, p. 41.
21. Brudholm, T. *Resentment's Virtue*, p. 29.
22. Langer, L. Quoted in Brudholm, T. *Resentment's Virtue*, p. 39.
23. Scott, J. *A Poetics of Forgiveness*, p. 199.
24. Scott, J. *A Poetics of Forgiveness*, p. 199.
25. Gobodo-Madikizela, P. *A Human Being Died That Night*, p. 118.
26. Gobodo-Madikizela, P. *A Human Being Died That Night*, p. 120.
27. Gobodo-Madikizela, P. *A Human Being Died That Night*, p. 127.
28. Gobodo-Madikizela, P. *A Human Being Died That* Night, p. 123.
29. Gobodo-Madikizela, P. *A Human Being Died That Night*, p. 123.

CHAPTER 10

# Re-imagining Forgiveness

Ever since I was ordained as a priest in 1987 I have felt the need to try to understand forgiveness; the word is so prominent in Christian liturgy and the idea so distinctive of Christian identity. I had studied both psychology and theology and yet neither seemed to have a real grip on the subject. I started reading what the philosophers and ethicists had to say and while some of that was very clear and precise I was still not satisfied that I was getting to the heart of the matter. I worked on a PhD and still felt myself to be in the foothills of the subject. Situations continued to arise which left me as tongue-tied as I had been before I ever started to reflect seriously on the subject. I got involved in all sorts of other things and developed other interests but the fundamental question of forgiveness haunted me. I thought it was just me, but some of my experiences and my wider reading convinced me that this was not so.

Forgiveness is both an enigma and yet something that we can be clearer and more positive about than we often are. The problem is that the truth about forgiveness is darker, more difficult and infinitely more agonizing than the myths about forgiveness which people, not least Christian people, prefer to promulgate. Yet behind this distressing truth is a deeper and more encouraging one. Fantasy forgiveness is actually of little use to anyone, whereas real forgiveness, which involves embracing not only the chaos out there but also the agony within, does have the capacity to heal.

Over a quarter of a century later a lot of water has passed under many bridges. The study of forgiveness has developed in a number of interesting, complementary and fruitful directions. The word is more regularly used and the possibility of forgiveness more generally entertained. The word 'forgiveness', which is about setting free, has itself been set free as events from the political changes in Eastern Europe and the end of apartheid to 9/11 have impacted on our moral imaginations and spiritual sensibilities.

As more and more has been published about forgiveness it has been difficult to keep up, and progress on this book has been often been delayed by my discovery of yet another interesting and important volume. Among them, Jill Scott's *A Poetics of Forgiveness* has been particularly helpful. 'Poetic' for Scott does not mean 'lyrical' or 'romantic' but refers to the importance of creativity. Just as forgiveness is itself 'created' so it brings into existence a new future in terms of identity, relationship and indeed community and nation than would otherwise be possible.[1] This emphasis on creativity has encouraged me to persist with what we might imagine as a wide-angled view of forgiveness. This involves not focusing in on a definition of forgiveness but opening up the lens to admit all sorts of insights, some of which look out of place from the perspective of one particular discipline – whether ethics, psychology, theology or any other.

Jacques Derrida states that we can only properly forgive the unforgivable and that such 'pure' forgiveness is 'mad'.[2] I find that idea very encouraging. The attempt to fit whatever we mean by forgiveness into the categories provided by rationalist ethics, psychology or theology seems to me to be a mistake.

If forgiveness is a reality then it is a vitally important one and needs to be creating the criteria by which other concepts and actions are judged. When Derrida says that forgiveness is mad what he means is that it cannot be calculated or normative but that it necessarily involves something new and unexpected.[3] This connects with the point that is often made that it is only those with the political, personal and spiritual freedom to be creative who can forgive.

True forgiveness cannot be formulaic. Pumla Gobodo-Madikizela argues that the forgiveness agenda has moved away from the question of this or that act of forgiveness, to the question of how a society may create the conditions in which forgiveness might flourish.[4] We could argue about the nature of these conditions and how much encouragement to forgive might be part of the mix, but the point is sound. If only the free and creative can forgive, and we think that forgiveness is a good thing, then our project is not to press people to forgive but to empower them to be free. And one way in which people can free themselves and others is through forgiveness. If this sounds circular, it is. Forgiveness and freedom together create a virtuous circle, or spiral. It is when we participate in this that we begin to contradict and overcome the contrary dynamic of violence, revenge and hatred. Forgiveness, then, is more dynamic than event. It is also a matter of the heart. It is a personal, practical and potentially political spirituality.

I myself have sometimes been described as 'box-ist' – I am allergic to putting things, be they people or ideas, into boxes or categories. This is perhaps one reason why I have been drawn to the study of forgiveness. If ever there was an anti-category concept, forgiveness is it. It is by definition against all forms of 'tying down' and 'closing off' and any commentary on the nature, meaning or practice of forgiveness should reflect this.

Try to fit forgiveness into any other ideology and it will seem 'mad'. Try to construct an ideology or philosophy of life on forgiveness and you will be seen to be 'mad' and less than fully moral. But the Christian belief is that to attempt to do so opens the door to real sanity, genuine freedom, true wisdom and the possibility of life being characterized by a peace informed by both justice and mercy.

## Creativity

The question driving the reflections in this book is based on the encounter with the mother of a murdered teenager. This is one way of articulating it: 'How might one human being be a good companion to one who has suffered some unjust catastrophe and yet who raises the question of forgiveness?' Within the sweep of that question I wish to imply the parallel one of 'and suppose that you yourself were the victim?' for the issues overlap to a significant degree. In a philosophical paper on forgiveness, Aurel Kolnai presented a very stark case that states that forgiveness is either unjustified or unnecessary.

His argument is that there is no space between condoning – which is wrong and not forgiveness – and responding to an offender who has fully repented and changed – which is not forgiveness so much as accepting that they have changed. He then goes on to consider the much messier and more realistic situation where the wrongdoer has not yet had 'a dramatic and fundamental change of heart' but where the offended person trusts that they will. In such cases he suggests that forgiveness is neither merely to condone what was wrong, nor to accept that the wrongdoer has changed but it is a 'generous venture of trust' through which the offender is 're-accepted'.

The study of forgiveness has moved on in many ways since Kolnai formulated things in this way but the idea of a generous venture of trust remains a vivid and valuable one. Kolnai's concern, like that of many philosophers, was particularly with the kind of situation which we described as level two in Chapter 2.[5] The harm done is unjust but without a disorienting emotional charge and well below the level of shattering violation. Put together with Scott's insights this leads me to suggest that it might be helpful to think of forgiveness as a generous *and creative* venture of trust.

Adding the word 'creative' to the description is important and is intended to move us away from the language of 'process' which, while based on the truth that forgiveness is rarely instant, is too constricting in its connotations. 'Process' accurately suggests that forgiveness takes time but implies something much more rational, controlled and controllable than I believe forgiveness to be. It also unhelpfully holds out the prospect of 'closure'. But it is not only Scott's approach which encourages me to see creativity as integral to forgiveness, James Alison's attempt to re-imagine forgiveness on the basis of a non-retributive theology takes exactly this step.

Alison's reflections on forgiveness begin in a very different place from my own but come to some very similar conclusions. His concern is how to address those gay Catholics who seek to forgive the church for its hatred of and violence towards gay people over the years. In particular, those who were so disappointed that no apology came in the millennium year and have since been vociferous in demanding one. Seeing this behaviour as reflecting patterns of violence and vengeance he argues that it is better that the Vatican should not apologize because there has not yet been a change of heart and that it would be better if any who desire to express forgiveness to the church should do so quietly and without fuss.

His concern characteristically is to have a non-violent form of forgiveness, one which does not involve the forgiver elevating him or herself and humiliating the forgiven. His concern is sound and overlaps extensively with the sorts of conclusions to which these reflections have brought us. For instance, he believes that a 'new "we"' is created by the pronouncement of forgiveness. Forgiveness can neither perpetuate an old 'us and them' nor create a new one. Alison's fundamental re-imagining is that forgiveness is not the last step in a process of overcoming harm, but the first. It is the forgiveness of the offended that allows, facilitates and encourages the change of heart of the offender.

Based as it is on his re-reading of the way in which atonement works,[6] the idea that forgiveness goes before repentance can be seen as an application of a theological perspective. If it were the case that humans forgive in the way that God forgives then this would all make sense. However, my own reflections suggest that human forgiveness, while a member of the same family of ideas as divine forgiveness, works very differently and so I would question the way he applies this to forgiveness between human beings or between individuals and institutions. More positively, his emphasis on the creativity needed by the forgiver is extremely helpful, as is his emphasis on the courage that is implicit in forgiving. He does not use the word 'courage' and would, I suspect, prefer the word 'faith'. While I would agree that the only faith worth having is that which inspires courage as well as other qualities, there is a need to underline the point that forgiveness is a risky business and that the risk is borne by the forgiver:

> Forgiveness in this model is precisely not a hermetic sealing-off from the other whom I declare myself to be nothing at all like. On the contrary, forgiveness turns out to be a creative moving towards someone *whom I am like* in such a way that they will be free from death *with me* so that together we will be a new 'we'. It is not a simple gesture or a pronouncement, but a living towards running the risk of being killed by the person, over time.[7]

There are lots of resonances here with the stories we have recounted of Marian Partington, Pumla Gobodo-Madikizela and Eric Lomax. Forgiveness involves generosity and trust, creativity and courage on the part of the forgiver. I am not taking Alison's 'new we' to mean 'reconciliation', rather a new sense of humanity on either side of the previous divide. At a human level this is not about the future of a relationship in the sense that the forgiver is in any sense obliged to live in close community or restored intimacy with the offender, but about the capacity to let a process of 'distasteful empathy' lead to a re-imagining of the humanity of the offender or violator.

## Not a Model but a Map

At one time I felt it should be possible to formulate a new and better step-by-step description of 'the forgiveness process'. But while there are some examples of forgiveness which do follow something like a textbook process I am convinced that this is not normal and that to promote such ideals is possibly to do more harm than good to those who most deserve our help. Some psychologists use such ideas and that is of help to many, but I suspect that the processes that are described often serve primarily to assist the helper in organizing the chaos that characterizes these sorts of situations. They also offer a framework for understanding which is good enough to help them manage their own anxieties and fears so that they might be a helpful listening companion to the victim who somehow, against all the odds, and against many of their gut feelings, hopes that forgiveness might emerge.

Although I have been persuaded against the possibility of any clear forgiveness process, there is some shape to what I envisage. What I have plotted is less a process, and certainly not a programme, but a very sketchy and diagrammatic map. The key feature on the map is the vast wilderness of hurt, into which the victim is cast by the violating offence. The wilderness is bounded on all sides by the river of distasteful empathy. On the far side of the water is land far less barren than the wilderness of hurt but which is, in every regard, different to the remembered paradise of the days before the violation. There is, alas, no possibility of return but this new land is a place where it is possible to flourish.

The generous and creative venture of forgiveness remains a project, even here. It would be naïve to say that this new country is a place where all are reconciled, but it is true that it is a place where both victim and perpetrator are psychologically and spiritually free from the violating offence. In the wilderness of hurt the victim carried the perpetrator around in a locked cell deep within their heart. As they cross the river of distasteful empathy the perpetrator is imaginatively freed and the cell door left ajar.

That is one way of picturing it. It is a three-phase venture in which the first phase is all about recovery and healing, the second about the kind of relationship that is desired with the perpetrator and the final and endless stage is the continuing journey of life. In this third phase, life is different because of the violation and because of the time in the wilderness and the crossing of the river.

What this is *not* is a three-step process of forgiveness which assumes that forgiveness in some sense happens and can be looked back on. Forgiveness of one person by another is always partial and vulnerable, even when it seems to be complete. The only thing that could change this would be the loss of memory. Yet something happens when the river is crossed and it is worth attending more closely to this part of the journey (provided it is not confused with the whole venture). Forgiveness, like love, is endless. Also like love, it can have its significant and transformative moments.

So, what happens as we cross the water from the wilderness of hurt to the new country where we continue the venture of forgiving? Although in much better shape than they were when first cast into the wilderness of hurt, most victims are not able to forgive simply by trying to forgive, by 'making an effort'. Although forgiveness can only happen when we desire it to happen, it cannot happen simply because we want it to happen. We cannot force ourselves to forgive anymore than a non-swimmer can make herself swim by dint of determination. So simply to cast oneself into the water is foolish and dangerous. What I believe is necessary here is for the victim to risk engaging in the distasteful empathy whereby they can begin to understand and appreciate something of the internal life of the perpetrator and the conditions which led to the violation. This is not, I repeat, so that the perpetrator can be excused, but so that they can be related to as a human being. To engage in distasteful empathy is to reach out to the most alien, despised and perhaps feared of others. This is necessary whether or not the perpetrator shows any signs of remorse or regret. Should they do so, however, only makes life a little easier and more palatable.

The agony is not removed by repentance any more than is the need for distasteful empathy and as the distasteful empathy is engaged so the victim gets drawn into the water only to find that it is the place of healing agony. As long as they are in that place, they are torn between the outrage of their own hurt and its consequences and the reality that the perpetrator is also a human being.

As the journey through the water continues, so the agony gets worse. The victim does not want to leave the wilderness of hurt, for there are consolations and satisfactions there. The perpetrator is locked away in that inner cell and the one thing that matters most to them – that their victimhood is honoured – is assured. In the wilderness of hurt, every victim is lonely. As they reach the other side so the key is turned in the door of that inner cell and the perpetrator-prisoner is released from their confinement and as the victim steps from the water, so she gives that now free prisoner a gift to add to the gift of freedom. It is the gift of her self as victim and so the perpetrator moves across the fertile plains of the new land bearing the burden of forgiveness, the victimhood of one whom he has made victim. It is a strange and yet life-giving burden, for it is the memory of having been forgiven.

It just remains to reinforce the final point in the understanding of forgiveness that I have developed. It is that forgiveness does not happen because we try to forgive. Forgiveness happens because three other things happen: (i) others reach out to us with empathy and that facilitates our healing – our journey to the edge of the wilderness of hurt; (ii) we reach out to the perpetrator with distasteful empathy and this leads us to healing agony by which we cross the water that makes the wilderness an island; (iii) we then stride out across the new land in the cause of justice and truth, mercy and peace. The result of this is forgiveness, that is to say, the giving away of our victimhood and the embarking on a new life with different but lighter vulnerability.

Looking back one might say that in a way, and to a degree that does *not* imply closure, forgiveness has happened. What we cannot say, however, is that *we* have *done* it or that it is complete. Forgiveness is not a personal achievement, though our intentions and capacities as victims and our responses to how others act are relevant. Forgiveness is not a step-by-step process. Some examples of forgiving can be understood exactly as the steps of a process but there is no such thing as 'normal' or normative process any more than there is a normal or normative life. Nor is forgiveness something that undoes the damage of the past. Hannah Arendt's famous concept that it deals with the problem of irreversibility is overstated.[8] Forgiveness is how we live *with* the problem of irreversibility. Forgiveness is a generous and creative venture of trust in the course of which the victim-self is given to the freed perpetrator and the true unburdened self is restored to itself.

## Forgiveness Emerges

Forgiveness is not the same as reconciliation. It might be that you fear getting into forgiveness because you think that if you forgive you have to relate to the person who caused the harm in the same way as before. That's not true and would be another way of suggesting that the clock might be turned backwards. Forgiveness always involves moving forward to a new way of being yourself and to new and renewed relationships. Forgiveness honours the hurt and the harm that was done, respects the violation or the death inflicted, but begins to hold these dreadful truths in the context of wider purposes and realties. The event is not forgotten but neither does it dominate the memory or the imagination.

Another metaphor might say that serious violation stops the clock, while forgiveness allows the clock to tick again. The time and the date of the violation then slip to where they belong, which is neither the present moment, nor oblivion, but the remembered past. The one who forgives is therefore free to live into the future, to cross the water at the edge of the wilderness and explore the new land. 'Textbook forgiveness' may lead to reconciliation but real and incomplete forgiveness probably will not and often should not and sometimes cannot. Forgiveness may often be better encouraged if we forget about reconciliation and focus on making the space for healing which may in turn liberate some distasteful empathy.

It may even be best, as I have already hinted, to forget about forgiving. That might sound odd because we are only considering the question of forgiveness because it has been raised by the victim. But I believe that one of the reasons that I said to the mother of the murdered boy (in Chapter 1) that 'it is far too early to talk about forgiveness' is because I felt that it would only make matters more difficult, complex and painful at a time when they were already overwhelmingly so. Forgiveness can be facilitated by taking our attention and imagination away from it for as long as we are in the wilderness of hurt. The challenge of distasteful empathy is just too great and too distasteful at this stage. Overwhelmed by our own suffering and pain we have no internal space for the other and yet we cannot forget them, which is why we lock up a horrible caricature of them in a secure prison cell within the imagination of our hearts.

But forgetting about forgiving is not only about the pragmatics of the wilderness of hurt; it might often be wise. We saw in Chapter 8 that the desire to forgive can go wrong in a number of ways: in particular through 'forgiveness boosterism' and the 'forgiver syndrome'. These are quite serious problems. There are other 'corruptions' of forgiveness which are also problematic – therapeutic forgiveness which essentially ignores the perpetrator is one. But what we might call 'repentance-dependent forgiveness' is another as it makes the victim a prisoner of the violator or offender until they have a change of heart and mind and this imposes on them a degree of obligation to forgive, which might be quite impossible if they are still lost in the wilderness of hurt and the perpetrator does not have the skill or inclination to find and meet them 'where they are'.

The desire to forgive is often caught up with the notion that the victim has some power over the perpetrator. I have already suggested that this derives from the inappropriate application of the analogy of divine forgiveness to the interpersonal situation. Pastoral theologian and pastor John Patton notices this when he analyses one of his own cases. He is talking with Tom who says he has a lump in this throat after talking on the telephone to his father. In the conversation the older man had 'shared some of his feelings of weakness and hopelessness prior to divorcing Tom's mother'. [9] This is a brief extract from the conversation with the pastor:

Pastor: What's the lump? Discovering that he had problems too?
Tom: Wondering if I really can forgive him.
Pastor: It's hard to give up that power.
Tom: Power?
Pastor: You sound more like a priest than a son. Go back to the lump in your throat.[10]

This is a good example of the way in which a 'forgiveness agenda', whether in the form of 'forgiver syndrome' or 'forgiveness boosterism' or the form it has here, which is to mistake yourself for one who has power to absolve, can get in the way of the distasteful empathy which is the only thing which can begin to initiate the healing agony which might issue in forgiveness.

Patton's interpretation of forgiveness is based not on the kinds of situation which have been most prominent in this book, that is the violating and shattering hurt by someone who is a stranger, but with the kinds of harm that occur within already established relationships. As we have seen already, these can be devastating and shattering partly because of the capacity of betrayal to undermine trust, but also because of the capacity of disappointment within intimate and family relationships to be seriously disturbing and disorienting and to erode self-confidence and self-esteem.

Disappointment can even threaten the integrity of the narrative which has so far been holding the self together.[11] So there is a good deal in common at a deeper level between these situations: the map of the territory – wilderness, water, new land – seems just as fitting with intimate betrayal as with shattering hurt.

I am inclined to align myself with Patton's view that forgiveness is not something that is done but something that is *discovered*. The relevant discovery, as far as Patton is concerned, is that the offender is 'human like myself':

> The problem with human forgiveness in special relations [his term for established family relationships and the like] is that when human forgiveness is understood as doing something or not doing something, it is virtually impossible to avoid being above or below the other or to escape the roles of priest and penitent – roles which maintain separation rather than facilitate intimacy.[12]

Patton therefore advocates forgiving, 'by not trying to'. Forgiveness is 'not something we have the power to do or are righteous in doing but a description of the nature of our now-and-to-come kingdom relationship to God and to one another'.[13] As I have said, I am very much inclined to see things like this, but Patton's point does not translate perfectly into the situations that we have described when the harm inflicted is overwhelming and the prior relationship minimal. So my conclusion is not that forgiveness is 'discovered' but that forgiveness *emerges*.

I don't believe that the situations that I have described can be expected to yield the discovery that 'deep down we are all the same' in the same way that more local or domestic examples might. That may well be part of it but I believe forgiveness will be discovered little by little, moving from 'impossible to imagine' to 'distasteful' to 'agonizing' and *en route* becoming healing. I am also not convinced that 'discovered' is a sufficiently open word. It implies something too much like closure, whereas the analysis here is that what becomes possible is the continuing process of forgiving, the ongoing beating of the forgiving heart as the water is crossed and the new land traversed. This is why I prefer to speak of forgiveness emerging as part of the character of the hurt but healed victim who has taken the decisive step into the water of distasteful empathy and then on to the new dry land of 'victim no more'.

Forgiveness is like love in that it comes only from the heart. Word and gestures might help communicate it, and might indeed help the forgiveness process along, but if the heart is not in it then it is not forgiveness. But forgiveness is also like happiness in that it is not usually found when it is directly sought. The most profound happiness is a kind of self-forgetfulness in joy which is found outside yourself – the delight in nature or a compelling task or in other people. Forgiveness also requires a degree of self-forgetfulness, a degree of humility, in order to flow.

People get into a muddle when they start to think of forgiving as something grand and to be declared from on high. True forgiveness comes from the heart and stands neither on ceremony nor on the supposed status of the victim. Indeed true forgiveness involves giving that victim status away – 'victim no more' is the tee-shirt slogan of the true forgiver. Forgivers are survivors, but they remain forgivers even though they are self-forgetful about their forgiving.

Forgiveness, then, will require every ounce of generosity, courage and creativity that can be mustered when we have been hurt. However, these are also some of the qualities needed to survive in the wilderness of hurt. The wise forgiver will recognize that forgiveness is impossible while lost in that desert and will use these qualities as 'survival skills' on their wanderings. Then, when it is at last possible to cross the water of distasteful empathy and to inhabit a better place, generosity, creativity and courage need to be directed to the new task.

It may not be wise to think of this as 'trying to forgive'. The task rather is 'to seek to relate to' the perpetrator. That, I believe, is as much as we can ever seek to do. Is that a strong enough ambition? Yes it is, because it is only those who seek to relate to the humanity of the one who has harmed, hurt, injured, betrayed or even violated them who will ever find that, somehow, forgiveness begins to emerge and that their heart beats in a new way as they walk the territory on the far side of the river of healing agony.

## Notes

1. Scott, J. *A Poetics of Forgiveness*, p. 3.
2. Derrida, J. *On Cosmopolitanism and Forgiveness*. Derrida's view is that we can only forgive the unforgivable.
3. Niva Arav makes this point very clearly in her essay 'To Exceed the Scene of Economy: Derrida's Forgiveness and Responsibility' in Bloch-Schulman, S. and White, D. (eds) *Forgiveness: Probing the Boundaries*.
4. See above p. 169
5. Kolnai, A. 'Forgiveness', p. 100.
6. The argument is that God's love is not organized for us through the processes of sacrifice. Rather, the passion death and resurrection of Jesus are a way of opening a way of life in which people can be free of the fear of death. See *On Being Liked,* Chapter 2.
7. Alison, J. *On Being Liked*, p. 42, (original emphasis).
8. Arendt, H. *The Human Condition*, p. 237ff.
9. Patton, J. *Is Human Forgiveness Possible?*, p. 74.
10. Patton, J. *Is Human Forgiveness Possible?*, p. 74.
11. This is another way of referring to the idea of 'shattering' which we explored as the highest level of hurt in Chapter 2.
12. Patton, J. *Is Human Forgiveness Possible?*, p. 172.
13. Patton, J. *Is Human Forgiveness Possible?*, p. 174.

CHAPTER 11

# A Forgiving Heart

This study has drawn attention to many aspects of the enigma of forgiveness. The primary concern has been what is possible for, and can be expected of, a person who is the victim of serious and unjust harm. Clearly, the situation is very different for those who are in the position of finding that the perpetrator has now repented of their actions. They regret what they have done and where possible seek to put right any injustice caused. This does change things for the victim.

But repentance cannot necessarily be taken at face value. The victim still needs to ascertain whether the repentance, regret and remorse are sincere and whether any restitution is appropriate and adequate. If they are, then the victim is in a position where forgiveness is, if not a duty, then something very close to a duty. There can be differences here depending on the moral code of the victim and their ethical community, but in terms of Christian ethics the situation is reasonably clear. The fully repentant perpetrator does not deserve to be forgiven but the victim should, to be a faithful Christian, seek to forgive them.

If that situation sounds stark it is in part because it is hypothetical. A real issue for the victim in these circumstances is in trying to ascertain how *sincere* such repentance is. It would be wise, in such cases, not to focus too much on the amount of emotion expressed. Histrionic regret is often more self-regarding than another-regarding and that is to fail to give the victim the respect that they need and deserve. True repentance is a change in me which is not all about me but all about my victims. Is my repentance sincere? I may believe it to be, but then I have first-hand knowledge of my own inner intentions that is not available to others. On the other hand, I may be able to deceive myself. The victim must make a judgement about my repentance and to do that they need, in the end, to engage their empathy for me, the one who hurt, harmed, injured or violated them.

Empathy is important when the offender is showing evidence of remorse and respect, but it also has a place when those significant ingredients are not present. This is a different place altogether, and much ethical ink has been spilt pursuing the question of whether or not forgiveness is just when there is no repentance. I have not given that question as much attention as some might think necessary because I do not believe it to be nearly as significant a question as is often argued. As I have already suggested, not only is the word 'repentance' problematic at the interpersonal level unless carefully defined and distinguished from the spiritual and religious meaning, but its presence or absence is never an open and closed case as far as the victim is concerned. I grant that it is different when there is not even a suggestion of a repentant attitude but that need not be the end of the matter in terms of forgiveness. A tragic situation can become a forgiveness story even in the absence of repentance. It may not be a story which is ever entirely concluded. Part of my argument here is that forgiveness stories are not judged only by their ending but by the subtle interplay of characters and events that make up a plot which has a trajectory in the direction of what we might call full or total forgiveness.

The number of cases in which anything like total forgiveness is ever achieved is probably over-estimated, partly for the ironic reason that spectacular examples of heroic and complete forgiveness are celebrated and repeatedly told: they become iconic and are mistakenly thought of as representative or typical precisely because they are exceptional. Also, for the more invidious reason that stories of partial forgiveness (which in no way intends to slur or demean them) are often passed on (or should I say, passed off) as complete and concluded forgiveness stories.

So, from my perspective, which is I believe both a credible Christian one, and one with which non-Christians might have a good deal of sympathy, there *is* a forgiveness agenda in situations where there is no manifest repentance. I would go on to say that there is also a forgiveness agenda where the primary victim has died and the relevant victim is a family member or close friend. There is also a forgiveness agenda in the case where the perpetrator is dead, or so distant as to be beyond communication – for instance in prison on a life sentence and refusing to receive any mail from victims or victims' families. The forgiveness agenda in these cases is summarized not by the question 'can I forgive him or her their crime', but 'how under these circumstances do I become a forgiving person?'. Or, 'how do I now retain or develop a forgiving heart?'

This is a question of immense personal and spiritual importance not only for victims but for all who might one day become a victim of serious and unjust harm. For the project of developing a forgiving heart is not one that we can leave until something traumatic happens to us and we inhabit for the first time the wilderness of hurt. It is an experience for which we need, in subtle and spiritual ways, to be prepared. The spirituality of forgiveness is not something to put off until we are thrust into the wilderness of hurt.

## The Qualities of a Forgiving Heart

Four distinct qualities are needed to make up a forgiving heart. No one person will ever have them all to a supreme degree. All can legitimately feel a sense of inadequacy here but the wise will take that as a spur to seek to develop these qualities. Some people will, however, be more naturally predisposed to forgive, while for others the qualities will not come easily. What, then, are the qualities that make up this cluster? First, there is a high degree of empathy, second an orientation towards the future, third, faith and fourth a concern about justice. These are all 'big words' and I will explain the way in which I mean them a little more fully, starting with justice.

In order to forgive we have first to know that there is something that needs to be forgiven. There are plenty of things that happen which might not be to our taste or which disappoint or distress us which cannot be forgiven precisely because there is nothing to forgive. When such things happen we need to be able to accept them and either ameliorate or tolerate their consequences for us. But, in order for forgiveness to be relevant and appropriate, whatever has caused us pain and distress needs to be unjust. It follows logically that the forgiving person must be attuned to the demands of justice.

Forgiveness is only relevant in the aftermath of injustice. However, to forgive is not simply to attend to the demands of justice or to write them off. The forgiving heart will therefore be attuned to the demands of justice and it may well seek to see justice done. But it will not do so in a vindictive way. Rather it will be concerned to liberate itself from the consequences of the unjustly inflicted hurt which we have summarized as 'victim status' and to release the perpetrator from its parallel which we might call 'perpetrator status'. In forgiveness both victim and perpetrator are returned to 'human being status'.

A sense of justice in the light of what has happened is thus a vital ingredient in the forgiving heart. But a forgiving person will be just as inclined to look forwards as to look backwards. One of the consequences of an unjust and hurtful event is that it attracts our attention and keeps us looking back, remembering the incident and examining its causes and consequences. The forgiving person will not, however, get stuck in this retrospective approach. Certainly they will be inclined and able to remember the event and will have a good deal of interest in why it happened. But the forgiving person will always have a strong disposition towards the future and this will impact on the way in which they will regard both the pain and the injustice.

People often connect the ideas and practices of restorative justice with forgiveness. One of the reasons for this is that restorative justice is very future-oriented. It is concerned with the changes that might make things better in the future rather than letting the future be determined by the past, which is in a sense what happens with retributive justice and punishment – especially punishment by custodial sentence. Restorative justice is not the same as forgiveness but they do share this future orientation and sometimes people might express forgiveness in restorative justice programmes.

One reason why restorative justice is controversial is that it can be demanding and stressful for the victim. In this way it is like forgiveness and so fits better in a worldview which understands that the 'forgiveness challenge' faced by victims is not an additional burden foisted on them by an uncaring society but part of the human condition under God, and so our attention turns to questions of faith. I am not going to argue that only Christian believers can be forgiving people, or that Christian people necessarily have forgiving hearts, but that forgiving people either have an overt or an implicit faith which resonates with the view that goodness is stronger than evil. This sentiment is expressed alongside a family of similar ideas in a prayer of Desmond Tutu:

> Goodness is stronger than evil;
> Love is stronger than hate;
> Light is stronger than darkness;
> Life is stronger than death;
> Victory is ours, through Him who loves us.[1]

This, or something like it, is the sort of faith that one finds in the heart of a forgiver. It is exactly this faith that is challenged and tested in the wilderness of hurt. The wilderness is the place where we come to feel that our life's story, or our nation's story, or maybe our friend's story, might not have a positive narrative drive at all. The wilderness is the place where we appreciate and understand the fragility of goodness, love and light. It is deeply etched into the Judeao-Christian mindset. This was the experience of the Hebrews in the desert. They wandered for a couple of generations, experiencing the deepest of doubts and giving them voice in complaint and grumbling.[2]

It was in the wilderness that Jesus was tempted by the devil, as he was invited to take the positive and direct path of power rather than the indirect and vulnerable way of grace.[3] After the example of Anthony in the third century, many made their way to the desert of Egypt precisely to engage in the extreme spiritual struggle which takes place when the props and supports of easy living are removed and the individual is exposed to raw loneliness. The wilderness is the place which makes us doubt whether goodness really *is* stronger than evil, love stronger than hate, light stronger than darkness and whether life is actually victorious over death.

It is in this wilderness that victims of unjust harm find themselves, as we have seen. Somehow, however, the person of a forgiving spirit will find that this faith survives in the desert, or is, perhaps, even kindled there. But whether it is overtly religious or not, such a faith is always *faith*. It is never certainty. The victim knows that there is real and raw power in evil, hatred, darkness and death. But if they have a forgiving heart they will suspect that this is not the whole story and decline to be subjected to their captivating power and become either bitter and passive victims or hate-filled avengers.

The fourth quality of the forgiving person is empathy. There is no escape from the importance of empathy in any consideration of forgiveness. Its absence, whether permanent or temporary, is often part of the cause of unjust harm or hurt or even violation and yet its presence is integral to any way forward that might be called forgiving. We have already seen that the empathy of the victim is more important than the 'repentance' of the offender because it is by empathy that the victim will decide whether the offender is sincere. But empathy also has a role in situations where there is no evidence of regret, remorse, restitution or a new respect for the victim by the offender.

Empathy is what enables the victim in some sense to understand why the perpetrator did what they did. It is always important to qualify this idea instantly and say that this does not mean that the path to forgiveness is created by a super effort of empathy which so explains the hurtful actions in terms of the sad and harsh life of the perpetrator that all is excused. The point does bear repetition: forgiveness is not excuse or exculpation any more than it is tolerance or acceptance. This is why it is important to stress that the forgiving heart will prize justice before all else, though not at the exclusion of all else.

The distinction here is between explanation and excuse. It is by empathy that the victim can begin to develop some sense of where the hurtful or violating action came from. The value of this is not that it explains away or justifies the behaviour, but that some kind of explanation is helpful to the victim because it begins to enable them to construct some kind of meaning out of what seems to be a meaningless and hopeless situation.

Empathy is not the only way in which such meaning might be constructed. Facts matter too, as do perceptions, but when empathy is engaged there is a deeper apprehension of the other's reality. This can begin to interact with the anger and resentment of the victim and initiate a spiritual and emotional development in a forgiving direction. Without empathy the victim could hear all the facts and at the end of it say 'but none of that justifies what they did to me', and they would be correct to say so.

It is the view that a court of law would take, uncomfortable as that might be to sensitive and empathic members of the jury. But forgiveness is different. It is the work and prerogative of the victim, not the state. In forgiveness the victim begins imaginatively to enter into the mind of the perpetrator and to see how it all fits together. They might not like what they see and reject the thought patterns as evil but without the cognitive, emotional and spiritual capacity to do this, *and* some real moral courage or audacity, the victim's response will never be of a kind that we might call forgiving.

The forgiving heart, then, is one where there is space for justice, for the future, for faith and, through empathy, for the one who caused the harm or who perpetrated the violation. Any actual forgiving involves all four of these dimensions or facets but will take on a different quality or feel depending on many contingencies. Among them is the personality and character of the victim.

It is unlikely that any person would have all these as perfectly balanced strengths of character but that is of no great significance. What is of great significance is if people lack any trace of these qualities. A person without a sense of justice is not going to be able to forgive but will be doomed to acquiesce and accept whatever is thrown at them. A person without some kind of orientation to the future is going to be locked in the pain and hurt of the past and never forgive. A person without faith in goodness is going to struggle to believe that the injustice that they have experienced can be overcome in a positive way and so remain captive to it and be inclined to rely on punitive or avenging responses. A person without empathy is going to find it impossible to get any sense of what might have been going on in the mind and heart of the person who hurt, harmed or violated them and so not be able to have any kind of explanation of it, nor will they be able to judge how to respond to any regret or remorse or repentance.

Justice, hope, faith: these are vital to human forgiveness. But greater even than these, and more fundamental, is the distasteful empathy that begins to break down the alienation caused by unjust, even shattering, hurt.

## Notes

1. I am grateful to Archbishop Tutu for permission to quote this prayer.
2. See, for example, Exodus 16.1-3, 17.1-3; Numbers 11.1-6.
3. See Matthew 4.1-11; Mark 1.12-13; Luke 4.1-13.

## CHAPTER 12

# The Gifts of the Wise

One of the main conclusions that I have drawn from this extended meditation on forgiveness is that there is going to be no simple resolution to the question: 'What does forgiveness mean?' and no one answer to the practical question: 'How do I forgive?' The word is too broad in its meaning and application to allow for either. We have seen that complete forgiveness is rare and yet that incomplete forgiveness, while itself a major spiritual challenge, is evidence enough of a forgiving heart.

The question which we turn to in this chapter is one of those which set us off to explore forgiveness in the first place: 'How might we best accompany and support someone who has suffered serious and unjust harm and who is not content to respond with hatred, bitterness or vengeance as the responses?' Or to put it another way: 'How do we help someone who has a forgiving spirit and intention but who, for the most understandable reasons, finds themselves so lost in the wilderness of hurt that the generous venture of forgiveness is completely off the horizon?'

The prospect is a daunting one and many would shrink from it, perhaps wishing that they had long ago trained as the kind of counsellor or therapist who would know what to do and say in such situations. The reality, however, is that no one really knows what to say and that the best help often comes, not from specialists, but from those who can make a personal connection and who proceed with all the vulnerability of a fellow traveller. The qualities needed to help others towards forgiveness are not the preserve of the few; many people have them. But they do need to be named and reflected upon because they are not always the first things that come to mind when we begin to think about how we might help someone else on their venture of forgiveness.

I have identified three clusters of gifts that are of enormous value when put in the service of supporting or caring for a victim of unjust harm, hurt or of violation. Thinking of them in terms of the three gifts that the wise men brought to the infant Christ is a way of holding them in mind. Also, to think that as we offer support to others we are, in a way, sharing in what the wise offer to the Christ-child strengthens and reinforces the value and the significance of these gifts which, until named, can perhaps seem too ordinary to be of transformative value. Yet that is exactly what they are.

## Gold

The first quality needed if we are to support someone facing a major forgiveness challenge is a sense of how little we know. Only an intellectually modest companion will be inclined and able to engage in the *listening* which is the first and primary need of a deeply and unjustly hurt victim (remember Eric Lomax's comments about Helen Bamber and her colleagues).[1] But modesty is only part of it. The listening must not only be open minded and accepting but also empathic. The good companion will make not so much an intellectual connection as an emotional one. They will listen to the feelings, to the heart, to the soul of the victim. This is vital because if forgiveness is to emerge it will be from the depths.

The heart that needs to be heard will not always say pleasant or interesting things. Bitterness, hatred and desire for revenge need not be encouraged but they should be listened to and accepted as part of the reality when they emerge. If they are in the heart already they need some way to escape and you, the companion, might be the one who can slowly draw off the poison. The companion will therefore need to be patient and accepting.

Such are the qualities of a good and patient listener. These qualities are the most profoundly helpful that any person who seeks to offer care can develop and nurture in themselves. They are what the bereaved, the dying, those in pain and those facing uncertainty or crisis or the breakdown of long-term relationships all need. But the good companion to someone who has been the victim of serious unjust harm needs to bring more to the situation than generic listening skills.

I have already written much about the importance of empathy in the forgiver, in particular the distasteful empathy of getting into the mind of the one who hurt or violated you. I have also emphasized the reality of healing agony, one aspect of which is the empathy which is open to the pain of both victim and perpetrator. For the victim, the task is to remember their pain and its injustice while making space for the perpetrator's explanation (not excuse) and some of the pain they now experience for having caused the pain: the sincerely guilty offender's remorse needs to be felt before it can be believed and accepted. The challenge to the victim's companion is possibly even greater. He or she must be open to the pain of both victim and perpetrator and at the same time be attentive to their own pain. The companion must remain real and human and yet not become numbed, fearful or fascinated when encountering what might be real depths of pain and cruelty.

The good companion will also be able to keep track and pace with various emotional journeys. Indeed the capacity not only to empathize but also to adjust to the emotional and spiritual pace of the victim, and to be willing to take a few steps backwards when they do, are some of the more subtle skills needed by any who seek to be good companions to those on a venture of forgiveness.

The gift of gold, then, is the capacity and willingness to engage in *multiple forms of empathy* and to accommodate to the *emotional* pace of the victim. The great danger facing the victim of a serious hurt, or shattering violation, is that they not only lose their sense of self but that they lose their *voice*. This loss of voice might take many forms. Absolute silence is one, but the tendency to pick up and use someone else's script is another. The greatest danger is that the victim merely reflects back the cruel and hateful voice of the perpetrator. This is the unfreedom of revenge. To help the victim avoid getting caught in such a cycle, the good companion will not merely offer the counter-script of performative forgiveness (you offend me, I forgive you – the presence or absence of repentance being a detail here) but will listen with empathy until the voice, freedom and creativity of the victim begin to return, and in their renewed identity they being to enjoy some refreshed freedom. When things get to this stage, the victim is beginning to get to the edge of the wilderness of hurt. At this stage the companion will seek to affirm their freedom and bear with them the burden of the remembered violation or offence, and at the same time, find a way to imagine and engage with the mind that inflicted the suffering.

Such deep, patient and multiform empathy is the gold which the good companion offers. It is a priceless and enduring gift. But what are the gifts of frankincense and myrrh? Frankincense is traditionally the gift that reminds us of the presence of God and which invites us to engage in prayer and praise. Myrrh is an ointment associated with suffering and death. The good companion is someone who, in the aftermath of serious and unjust harm, will also bring frankincense and myrrh.

## Myrrh

Let's first consider myrrh. Like the gold there is more than one aspect to this gift. It has several dimensions, all of which are equally important. Those who have been seriously and unjustly harmed will have had, to a greater or lesser degree, a brush with evil. This is part of the shock and the trauma of it. Something has happened which really should not have happened and this unjust and evil aspect has probably had a deeper impact on them than either they or you realize. We are dealing here with the consequences of evil. Not the traditional, logical 'problem of evil', but the practical problem of the dealing with the damage that evil inflicts. If the evil has been expressed violently, say in a bombing or a personal physical attack or maybe over years of abuse, then the physical and emotional consequences will be difficult and painful to live with on a day-by-day basis.

But the spiritual level is important too. When I was helping a local community to cope with the murder of the teenage boy I mentioned in Chapter 1, I went to see a priest living about fifty miles away for some support. He suggested that I look at a collection of essays entitled 'The Fascination of Evil'.[2] As it happens, I was not in the mood for serious study but the title said a great deal to me. Evil carries a dangerous fascination, not least to those who are its victims. But companions are vulnerable too. Anyone supporting a person who has been the victim of something which might be described as evil is in danger of getting sucked in. So a companion of someone who has been seriously and unjustly harmed needs to bring with them a degree of awareness about the fascination and attractiveness of evil. This is especially true for people, both victims and their supporters, who have high levels of empathy.

Part of the journey will often involve seeking to understand why a person behaved in the way they did. There is a danger in that the psychopath will never be able to empathize with the victim but the victim might be able to get into the mind of a psychopath. That is, to allow psychopathic thought processes to run around inside their own head. Real wisdom and discernment is needed here. The need is to understand but also to be sure that you *don't* understand; to keep some distance from the thought processes which issue in harmful and damaging action. To fail to do so will at the very least begin to move the dynamic away from forgiveness and towards vindictiveness and revenge. Every victim should at some point remember that today's perpetrator is often yesterday's victim; and then think of their own tomorrow.

I recall very vividly a conversation I had one day over lunch with a theologian in New York. We were talking about reconciliation after violent conflict but the point applies very much to forgiveness. He was keen to impress upon me the importance and significance of what he called 'absorbing evil'. I felt that the idea made sense. We are familiar with the thought that one bad action leads to another. We have seen it happen, and been part of the process ourselves. Someone is rude to us so we are less sensitive in how we reply to them than we might be, and that leads to a drop in respect towards other people, so we are then rude to someone else who in turn passes that on... That's at the level of words. When it comes to physical violence it is much the same. In a dark twisting of the proverb that one good deed deserves another, the rule seems to be that once one party gets violent others see it as their task to take revenge.

'Retaliation' is the word, and it is derived both literally and in spirit from the ancient law of the *lex talionis* – 'an eye for an eye and a tooth for a tooth'.[3] To be fair to the law it is intended as a way of ameliorating the escalation of violence that so often happens when people adopt a revenge mentality – a vengeance mindset. The law means *only* one eye for an eye... That's a start, but such a law can never deliver forgiveness. The forgiving person needs to venture much further than that in generosity of spirit. One advantage that the law has over forgiveness, however, and one reason why forgiveness is so difficult, is that it does at least mean that something happens to deal with the evil. The evil goes somewhere. Indeed it goes straight back from whence it came. 'Return to Sender' is the message on the envelope of retaliation, however constrained.

Forgiveness is different. Forgiveness means that somehow the evil that was behind and perhaps in the harm, especially if it is shattering violation, needs to be absorbed and either neutralized or transformed. In that lunchtime conversation I was impressed by the thought, and moved by the idea that it might be so: that human beings might somehow absorb, neutralize or transform the evil that is thrown at them by others. Helping someone to do this is one of the more demanding and important challenges facing supporters and companions of victims. It has its risks, to be sure, but to fail to do it is also dangerous.

Myrrh not only points to suffering, and by implication the evil origins of unjust suffering, but also to death. Death is something which is relevant in two ways on the rugged terrain which we travel with victims. In some cases we are dealing with death quite literally: the death of a loved one or friend through murder. Anyone who would be a companion to someone close to a murder victim must have some familiarity with the valley of the shadow of death. Bereavement is never simple but bereavement after murder has all the complications of ordinary bereavement plus many more. The good companion will need to share in the slow process of acceptance of deep loss as well as, and in addition to, all the other issues that we have mentioned.

The future death of the surviving victim might not be at the forefront of our minds in these circumstances but it is highly significant. In the aftermath of serious harm the victim knows that one of the fundamental struggles is the way in which the event is going to impact on them for the *rest of their life*. We have seen that 'closure' after shattering events is often not a realistic hope; something raw and painful will always remain in the heart of the victim. The good companion must be alert to the extreme unlikelihood of closure. Sometimes people say things like 'you might forgive but you will never really get over it'. Other people speak of total or complete forgiveness, suggesting that there are ways in which it is possible to move on in a radial and thoroughgoing way.

Rather than firm up his or her personal opinions about such matters, however, it might be advisable for a companion to recognize that one of the features of the immediate aftermath of serious harm is a disorientation which prevents any clear thinking about the medium- or long-term future. The reality of what has happened, like pain, demands attention and draws in our horizon to the very immediate. It is almost inevitable that, when a shattered victim risks thinking into the future, they will see only the extension of the present moment in all its bleakness, distress and disorientation. To the victim of serious or shattering harm, the wilderness of hurt apparently extends to the horizon, no matter how far one travels. In such circumstances, the companion who believes in forgiveness needs to be extremely patient and circumspect.

A positive orientation to the future is a crucial quality of the forgiving heart, but the imagined future may well be a place of dread and despair. So to introduce the thought that forgiveness might somehow make the future more bearable has the capacity to feel not only insensitive but offensive. 'After such knowledge', wrote T. S. Eliot 'What forgiveness?' and many victims of shattering harm or atrocity have echoed the sentiment.[4] The good companion will need to realize that forgiveness, while some part of the shattered self desires to offer it, will simultaneously feel impossible and from time to time undesirable. What it might mean to forgive may be absolutely beyond the victim's imagination, and suggesting forgiveness in a clumsy way or at the wrong time might be the least helpful thing that can be said or done.

Quoting Jacques Derrida is not very likely to help a friend in distress, but his apparently irresolvable paradox (he calls it an 'aporia') should be borne in mind by the companion: 'forgiveness forgives only the unforgivable. One cannot, or should not, forgive; there is only forgiveness, if there is any, when there is the unforgivable.'[5] It may also help the companion of the victim who feels that they are 'going mad' to remember that, according to Derrida, it is forgiveness that is mad – in the sense that it is an unexpected and creative way forward which cannot be imagined outside an actual situation. These are subtle points but such 'advice' will be infinitely be more helpful than that based on Nietzsche's, 'what doesn't kill me makes me stronger'.[6] The companion's task is not to look for the positive benefits in unjust harm but to share in the pain and outrage and let the victim set the pace.

How then does this connect with death? The answer is that one of the tasks of the good companion to a victim is to hold for them the period between the limits of their current imagination and the end of their life. That might be many decades but for the victim it might also be a black hole. I have already mentioned patience as part of the golden gift of empathic listening. But with the gift of myrrh comes a sense of timing. One of the fascinating insights in Mary Foley's story as told by the Forgiveness Project is that she did not think about forgiveness in the first few days after the fatal stabbing of her daughter.[7] That it arose from within her made it far more likely that the story unfolded as a genuine forgiveness story.

Forgiveness can never be forced without losing its true quality. A victim can never be manipulated into 'forgiving' without being further abused. This truth suggests a further role that a companion might have: to keep their friends at some distance from the questions of journalists and people with a desire to help them forward according their own idea of what is appropriate in the circumstances. Victims need protecting from those who appear sympathetic but who have learnt to act in a concerned way to disguise their lack of concern. The good companion will not only be a good listener but will be a good gatekeeper, screening out bad listeners and people with big personal agendas, however well-meaning such people might be.

Those who want to preach forgiveness are not necessarily the best companions to victims. Rather, it is those who are able to empathize to the point that they too experience the healing agony of impossible but longed-for forgiveness and who have the spiritual stamina for the long journey ahead; those who know in a deep way the truth of George Herbert's couplet, 'but above all, the heart/must bear the longest part'. Forgiveness is not so much a journey, since journey implies destination, as a venture. In fact, as I suggested in Chapter 7, it can helpfully be seen as *spirituality*. Good companions to victims are therefore *de facto* spiritual guides.

## Frankincense

Frankincense is the gift that speaks of the presence of God. The companion or supporter who brings incense will be helping to open the victim up to what one might call the 'God dimension'. It is not necessary, of course, to bring God into a situation, for God needs no introduction to victims. They, like the poor, the frail and children are God's special friends. Nonetheless, victims might need to be reminded and reassured about God and God's involvement. However, the first task of the companion bearing incense is to remind the victim that they are not God. This might sound odd, or even harsh, but it is a first principle of good living, which is integral to the virtue of humility, to appreciate that I am not God.

There is a strong tradition which says that 'only the victim can forgive'. ('Forgiveness to the injured does belong', wrote John Dryden in the seventeenth century.) This generates great problems for anyone who seeks forgiveness for being the cause of someone else's death. It is a strong feature of Jewish teaching as several contributors to Simon Wiesenthal's Symposium after *The Sunflower* have argued. The helpful companion to a living victim, or bereaved relation of someone who has been killed, will not encourage the victim to take this quite at face value, however. For the message is not to the victim but to the offender. It does not and cannot mean that the victim has a power that would otherwise reside with God. Nor that the way in which victims forgive is like the way in which God forgives.

God forgives not as victim but as the origin and source of all the energy that is directed towards the coming of God's kingdom, where justice, truth, peace and mercy are held in perfect balance, and where people live in a fellowship of self-giving love. God forgives those who truly repent because to repent is to align oneself with the values, purposes and energies of God. God's forgiveness is instant because the work that needs to be done is not in the heart of God, which is always poised lovingly with regard to every human being, but in the heart of the repentant sinner. This work, the work of aligning oneself with God's nature, love, purposes and plans is immensely difficult for human beings and so the potential instantaneousness of God's forgiveness is rarely realized.

But the problem here is very different from that where the forgiveness is potentially between a victim and a perpetrator, where the change in the perpetrator that is required is only analogously called 'repentance' and where the change of heart in the victim which we call forgiveness is a major, ongoing and time-consuming piece of work involving the mind and the emotions, the heart and the soul, indeed the whole person; and which may or may not be initiated by the 'repentance' of the perpetrator.

The victim's companion will want, at the right time, to help the victim to realize that whatever attitude they adopt towards the offender that is not the last word regarding the offender's guilt or innocence either in law or in the sight of God. Gordon Wilson was clearly open-minded about the way in which God might judge the Enniskillen bombers. That open-mindedness was perhaps part of what enabled him to adopt a forgiving attitude ('I bear no ill will, I hold no grudge'). Wilson had the humility to know that he was nether God nor 'judge and jury' with regard to the bombers.

Many victims aggravate their own suffering and militate against the possibility that they might develop a forgiving attitude because they fear that as soon as they move in that direction it is as if the person is let off scot free. It cannot be said too often that justice and pardon belong to the state, justice and absolution to God and that the victim's choices are between tolerance, vengeance and forgiveness. When put like that the wisdom of the path of forgiveness begins to become clear. But true forgiveness cannot ever be forced for it is freedom, life and spirituality in the aftermath of unjust hurt.

The point, so rightly emphasized in Jewish teaching, is that if you have offended against your neighbour, perhaps by stealing from them, then it is inappropriate to go to God for forgiveness rather than to the neighbour. The point is plain and there is nothing in Christianity to contradict it. Indeed the point could be developed to say that if you have stolen from your neighbour it is no use going to them with a story of regret and a request to be forgiven if you are not prepared to restore the stolen goods. The good companion of a victim might sometimes be in the position of reminding of them of this. The remorse of the perpetrator is not always enough. Oddly it is with relatively low levels of harm, such as theft, that this is most clearly the case. When it gets to higher levels a different logic applies because the loss that has been incurred, for example of a murdered child, or the damage that has been inflicted, perhaps by violent attack or rape, is irreversible and beyond recompense. There are debts that cannot be repaid and that is one reason why forgiveness is ultimately more important than justice.

## Reflection

A victim who might one day be able to engage in forgiving, needs the support of those who will bring a number of gifts which I have grouped together under the headings of the three gifts that the magi brought to the Christ child. First there is the gold of empathic and patient listening. Then there is the myrrh which combines resilience to the attractiveness of evil, confidence in the company of suffering and death and the capacity to hold and contain the future in a positive and non-frightening way. Finally, there is the frankincense which knows the difference between God's forgiveness and that which any victim might offer and which is alert to the part which expressions of remorse, regret and restitution can play in different circumstances.

Above all else, the victim needs to know that they cannot forgive in that declaratory, definitive and absolving way that belongs to God alone and which blots out all traces of sin and evil. That power is simply not available to human beings. It may not even be available to God, if God cannot eradicate what the victim still resents. The still smouldering victim might find this an attractive notion and want to retain their resentment in order to consign the perpetrator to hell. The thought is far from impossible. But the price to be paid for such a strategy is extremely high. For just as it is a way of keeping the perpetrator out of God's kingdom, so it is a way of keeping the victim and the perpetrator bonded together.

This is an aspect of being a victim of someone else's harshness or cruelty that is deeply tragic and far more important than is often appreciated. Victim and perpetrator might have been strangers before the offence but they are connected by it and in its aftermath. The only thing that can break that connection is the forgiveness of the victim.

At the profoundest level this is why forgiveness is the most enlightened form of self-interest for when forgiveness happens both the perpetrator and the victim are unbound. This is one of the reasons why forgiveness and reconciliation, which are so often confused, must be distinguished. The one frees the tragically connected; the other connects the recently freed. Yet true forgiveness can never come from *pursuing* self-interest. It comes from the self-giving venture of distasteful empathy leading to the unlocking of the prison cell within and the giving away of the victim-self. However, as the self-as-victim is given away in forgiveness, so the self-as-victor emerges from the river of healing agony.

It is the vocation of a victim's companion, whether family member, friend, priest, counsellor, teacher, social worker or any other good neighbour, to seek to facilitate this transformation by offering their gifts to the victim; gifts that might help him or her with a generous and creative venture across the wilderness of hurt, the river of healing agony and then on into a land where newness of life and love are sustained by the forgiving hearts of those who are victims no more.

## Notes

1. See above, pp. 35–6.
2. Tracy, D. and Haring, H. 'The Fascination of Evil'.
3. Exodus 21.24; Leviticus 24.20; Deuteronomy 19.21.
4. The struggle with the possibility of future, or any meaningful sense of 'after', is explored in depth in the collection of essays edited by David Patterson and John K. Roth *After-Words: Post-Holocaust Struggles with Forgiveness, Reconciliation, Justice.*
5. Derrida, J. *On Cosmopolitanism and Forgiveness*, pp. 32–33.
6. See Chapter 2, p. 25.
7. http://theforgivenessproject.com/stories/mary-foley-england/.

# Bibliography


Alison, J. *On Being Liked* (London: DLT, 2003).

Arendt, H. *The Human Condition* (Chicago: University of Chicago Press, 1958).

Bash, A. *Forgiveness and Christian Ethics* (Cambridge: Cambridge University Press, 2007).

Bash, A. *Just Forgiveness Exploring the Bible, Weighing the Issues* (London: SPCK, 2011).

Bishop, B. '"The Visage of Offence": A Psychoanalytic View of Forgiveness and Repentance in Shakespeare's Plays', *British Journal of Psychotherapy* 23(1): 2006, pp. 27–36.

Bloch-Schulman and White, D. (eds) *Forgiveness: Probing the Boundaries* (Oxford: Interdisciplinary Press, 2009).

Brudholm, T. *Resentment's Virtue: Jean Améry and the Refusal to Forgive* (Philadelphia: Temple University Press, 2008).

Butler, J. *Butler's Fifteen Sermons Preached at the Rolls Chapel and a Dissertation on the Nature of Virtue* (London: SPCK, 1970).

Cassidy, S. *Audacity to Believe* (London: DLT, 1992).

Cavanaugh, W. T. *Torture and Eucharist* (Oxford: Blackwell, 1998).

Davidson, M. *Sorry: The Hardest Word and How to Use It* (London: Constable, 2010).

Derrida, J. *On Cosmopolitanism and Forgiveness,* trans M. Dooley and M. Hughes (New York: Routledge, 2001).

Dorfman, A. *Death and the Maiden* (London: Nick Hern Books, 1992).

Flanigan, B. *Forgiving the Unforgivable: Overcoming the Bitter Legacy of Intimate Wounds* (New York: Macmillan, 1992).

Garrard, E. and McNaughton, D. *Forgiveness* (Durham: Acumen, 2010).

Gobodo-Madikizela, P. *A Human Being Died That Night: A South African Story of Forgiveness* (New York: Houghton Mifflin Company, 2003).

Gobodo-Madikizela, P. and Van Der Merwe, C. (eds) *Memory, Narrative and Forgiveness: Perspectives on the Unfinished Journeys of the Past* (Newcastle: Cambridge Scholars Publishing, 2009).

Griswold, C. L. *Forgiveness: A Philosophical Analysis* (Cambridge: Cambridge University Press, 2007).

Haber, J. G. *Forgiveness* (Savage, MD: Rowman and Littlefield 1991).

Holloway, R. *On Forgiveness* (Edinburgh: Canongate, 2002).

Jones, L. G. *Embodying Forgiveness: A Theological Analysis* (Grand Rapids, MI: Eerdmans, 1995).

Kolnai, A. 'Forgiveness' *Proceedings of the Aristotelian Society 74*, 1973–1974, pp. 91–106.

Kraybill, D. B., Nolt, S. M. Weaver-Zercher D. L. *Amish Grace: How Forgiveness Transcends Tragedy* (San Francisco, CA: Jossey Bass, 2007).

Lamb, S. and Murphy, J. G. (eds) *Before Forgiving: Cautionary Views of Forgiveness in Psychotherapy* (Oxford: Oxford University Press, 2002).

Lewis, C. S. *Mere Christianity* (London: Fontana, 1952).

Lomax, E. *The Railway Man* (London: Vintage, 1995).

McCabe, H. *God, Christ and Us* (London: Continuum. 2003).

McFadyen, A. and Sarot, M. *Forgiveness and Truth: Explorations in Contemporary Theology* (Edinburgh: T & T Clark, 2001).

Mackintosh, H. R. *The Christian Experience of Forgiveness* (London: Nisbet, 1927).

Minow, M. *Between Vengeance and Forgiveness: Facing History after Genocide and Mass Violence* (Boston, MA: Beacon Press, 1998).

Nouwen, H. J. M. *The Return of the Prodigal Son: A Story of Homecoming* (New York: Doubleday, 1992).

Nussbaum, M. C. *Upheavals of Thought: The Intelligence of Emotions* (Cambridge: Cambridge University Press, 2001).

Partington, M. *Salvaging the Sacred: Lucy, My Sister* (London: Quaker Books, 2004).

Partington, M. *If You Sit Very Still* (Bristol: Vala Publishing Cooperative, 2012)

Patterson, D. and Roth, J. K. *After-Words: Post-Holocaust Struggles with Forgiveness, Reconciliation, Justice* (Washington: University of Washington Press, 2004).

Patton, J. *Is Human Forgiveness Possible? A Pastoral Care Perspective* (Lima OH: Academic Renewal Press, 2003).

Robinson, M. *Gilead* (London: Virago, 2005).

Robinson, M, *Home* (London: Virago, 2008).

Sacks, J. *Covenant and Conversation: A Weekly Reading of the Jewish Bible* (London: Maggid Books, 2009).

Scott, J. *A Poetics of Forgiveness: Cultural Responses to Loss and Wrongdoing* (New York: Palgrave McMillan, 2010).

Self, D. *Struggling with Forgiveness: Stories from People and Communities* (Toronto: Path Books, 2003).

Shaffer, P. *The Gift of the Gorgon* (London: Viking, 1993).

Spencer, G. (ed.) *Forgiving and Remembering in Northern Ireland: Approaches to Conflict Resolution* (London: Continuum, 2011).

Stephenson, S. *The Long Road* (London: Methuen Drama, 2008).

Swinton, J. *Raging with Compassion: Pastoral Responses to the Problem of Evil* (Grand Rapids, MI: Eerdmanns, 2007).

Tracy, D. and Haring, H. 'The Fascination of Evil' *Concilium* Volume 1, 1998.

Tutu, D. *No Future without Forgiveness* (London: Rider, 1999).

Twenge, J. M. and Campbell, W. K. *The Narcissism Epidemic: Living in the Age of Entitlement* (New York: Free Press, 2009).

Vitz, P. C. and Meade, J. M. 'Self-forgiveness in Psychology and Psychotherapy: A Critique'. *Journal of Religious Health* 50(20): 2011, pp. 248–263.

Volf, M. *Exclusion and Embrace: A Theological Exploration of*

*Identity, Otherness and Reconciliation* (Nashville, TN: Abingdon, 1996).

Watts, F. and Gulliford, L. (eds) *Forgiveness in Context: Theology and Psychology in Creative Dialogue* (Edinburgh: T & T Clark, 2004).

Wiesenthal, S. *The Sunflower: On the Possibilities and Limits of Forgiveness*, Revised and Expanded Edition (New York: Schocken Books, 1998).

Williams, C. *He Came Down From Heaven and The Forgiveness of Sins* (London: Faber and Faber, 1950).

Wilson, G. and McCreary, A. *Marie* (London: Marshall Pickering, 1990).

Wright, N. T. *Evil and the Justice of God* (London: SPCK, 2006).

# Acknowledgements

I have been thinking about forgiveness for so long that a comprehensive list of everyone who has taught me something about it would add another chapter to this book. Therefore I must ask many to forgive me for not mentioning them and restrict my explicit thanks to those who have helped me write this book.

I am fortunate in having local friends who have published in this area, among them Anastasia Scrutton and Anthony Bash, both of whom have been challenging conversation partners and positive supporters as I have sought to give voice to my own concerns and perceptions in this area.

I am aware that I have learnt a great deal from people who have been much closer to some of the painful realities that I describe than I would ever want to be. Tony Wright of Freedom from Torture (formerly Medical Foundation for the Care of Victims of Torture) has helped me to understand what shattering experiences do to people. Paul Tyler has given me glimpses into some of the issues he faces as chaplain at a high security prison. Marian Partington has not only educated me but has also inspired me through her writing and conversation and I am especially grateful for permission to quote from some of her as yet unpublished work.

In 2011 the Trialogue Conference, which brings together professionals from the worlds of spirituality, psychotherapy and literature, focused on the novels of Marilynne Robinson to which I refer, *Gilead* and *Home*. The insightful comments of many there, and the quality of attentive engagement with intractable issues connected with forgiveness, had a profound effect on the writing of this book. I am very grateful to have had the privilege of participating - and of learning so much.

Judy Turner, Anne Lindsley, Chris Taylor and Maggie Cherry have been kind enough to read and comment on draft chapters well before they should have been seen by anyone. Their comments were enormously helpful in enabling me to craft a book. Marina Cantacuzino, Director of the Forgiveness Project, has kindly given me permission to quote from the Forgiveness Project's website. Colleagues in the diocese and at the Cathedral in Durham have taken an encouraging interest in this project and been sympathetic when it has all seemed too much. Caroline Chartres at Continuum has been long-suffering in allowing the deadline for the project to creep on into the future and both kind and wise in her editorial suggestions.

To all these and my many unnamed mentors, I offer my sincere thanks.

George Herbert once wrote that 'the heart must bear the longest part'. This is true about forgiveness, or forgiving, in many ways. But it is also true of life's journey in marriage which is why I dedicate this book to Maggie, with heartfelt thanks and love.

# Index

*Index*

## Index